TAMING YOUR
STUPID MONSTER

BARRY W. WOLCOTT MD

TABLE OF CONTENTS

ACKNOWLEDGMENTS

This book is a reality only because of the help I received from many people.

My wife, Sue Ellen E. Wolcott is the ship's ballast stabilizing my family and my career; without her, those ships would have foundered many times.

Dr. William Lloyd MD, an early student and long-time friend and colleague, applied the bursts of subtle pressure and encouragement needed to keep my nose firmly at the grindstone over the whole writing and publishing process.

Dr. Lori Stone Handelman PhD, my editor at Clear Voice Editing (professionalnoveleditors.com), extracted the best from within my often convoluted prose while retaining my core thoughts and my author's voice.

Dan Berkowitz and his staff at AuthorPop (AuthorPop.co) transformed my e-manuscript computer file into a professionally formatted book and created an accompanying effective on-line presence for my work.

PREFACE

Stupidity is frequently the go-to element of successful comedy, but it burdens us individually and collectively; doing less stupid stuff would enhance both our personal and professional lives. I wrote this book specifically to help people "do less stupid stuff" in all aspects of their lives.

My career path has been marked by a series of high-stakes military and civilian roles; in each role, those with whom I worked were intolerant of stupid decisions. To succeed, I needed to minimize making them. To that end, I systematically reviewed my personal decision processes and took steps to identify and remove—or to compensate for—flaws that led me to make stupid choices.

In my roles as a worker and as a leader in the civilian and military healthcare ecosystems, as a healthcare advisor to non-medical senior executives, and as an entrepreneur, I have worked with novices, rookies, and old hands. I've had the opportunity to observe their flawed decision-making and have incorporated those lessons into modifying my own behaviors.

As a result of this self-study and the study of others, I have deliberately identified and honed a skill set that allows me to recognize when I may be about to make a potentially stupid decision, and to then heed that warning by considering before acting. As a result, I now "do far less stupid."

Most importantly to you as a reader, I have repeatedly succeeded in passing this skill set on to colleagues and subordinates in both military and civilian settings. As a result, their careers have been less burdened by the unwanted consequences of their own stupid decisions. This book makes that skill set available to you and provides you opportunities to adopt, and to adapt, its elements to your unique personality and setting. Within the flow of the book you will find exercises that will help you improve specific skills. Exercises identified as "To Improve Now" will help you internalize key issues as they apply specifically to you, and to better understand future material; these exercises will prove most useful if you complete them as you encounter them. Exercises identified as "To Improve Later" encourage integrating the book's concepts and honing the discussed skills within your day-to-day setting over time. They are best started as you reach them during your reading, and completed within the period recommended with each exercise.

In the book's first chapters, I present, in detail, this skill set and discuss how you can make use of its elements. In the second section, I relate and discuss a series of real-life examples; each one highlights one or more specific "stupidity avoidance skills" identified and discussed in the book's first section and provides skill-building exercises to imprint them. The third section presents fifteen real-life case study examples that illustrate the principles in action.

The examples share a unifying backdrop: each of the fifteen examples occurred during the five years I served as commander of the Army's hospital at the United States Military Academy at West Point, New York. While they share this common context, each example portrays specific, transferable, generic and universal lessons that are directly applicable to your personal efforts to reduce stupid decisions. Each example is directly supportive of this book's two central themes:

- The ability to avoid stupid decisions is not inborn; it is the end product of the deliberate and studied application of the skill set this book will help you master.
- Avoiding stupid decisions by routinely using this skill set will make you more effective in your personal and professional endeavors.

This is a "how to" book. Employing its lessons, you will:

- Recognize the presence of your personal Stupid Monster.
- Treat that recognition as a warning, just as you would the barking of a watch dog.
- Heed that warning by deliberately evaluating alternative options.
- Avoid the consequences of an initial (stupid) impulse.

By so acting, you will do less stupid yourself and reduce the time spent dealing with stupid's aftermath.

You will have tamed your Stupid Monster.

PART ONE

ME AND STUPID AND YOU

CHAPTER ONE

ME AND STUPID: A
LIFE JOURNEY

My efforts to identify, strengthen, and implement the skills that now help me avoid making stupid decisions—and teach those skills to others—occupied twenty years of my life. This journey eventually led me to present a series of lectures to medical students in which I conceptualized a "Stupid Monster" within us, and presented a series of lessons designed to minimize the frequency of its bite. One of those students, now a senior clinician, recently told me that those lectures had eased his road to success, and suggested I might turn them into a blog, a podcast, or even a book. His comments set in motion my writing the initial draft of this book.

My life journey with stupid is divided into four periods.

Period One
Mark Twain, Me, and Stupid

I was a new Army major, a physician in the Army Medical Corps, working at Walter Reed General Hospital in Washington, and in the last months of my three-year internal medicine residency. The Army Surgeon General's office informed me that I was to get my dream job: I would be joining the teaching faculty of the internal medicine residency at Brooke Army Medical Center (BAMC) in San Antonio, Texas.

This was a big deal! Such a faculty assignment normally comes only three to five years after residency, and then, only if the physician's performance in routine clinical assignments at one or two smaller Army hospitals demonstrated clear merit. In four months, I would be expected to oversee, teach, and supervise residents who had only a year less medical experience than I. They would surely be skeptical of someone with as little experience as I would bring with me. I imagined their recurring question would be, "How much can he possibly teach me?"

One reason I received this plum assignment was that the BAMC residency director, Colonel Andre J. Ognibene, MD, personally requested it. He had been one of my faculty supervisors at Walter Reed, and had quickly become a close mentor. When I called Dr. Ognibene to thank him for making the assignment possible, I also asked him what I could do to be best prepared. I expected him to suggest I create a series of formal presentations on specific medical issues to present to the residents, and so appear "scholarly."

Instead, he said, "You have all the medical skills you'll need to start this job and you're a good teacher; if, during your first year here, you can avoid appearing stupid, you'll do fine. Read and take to heart what Mark Twain said about looking stupid. He may not have actually said it, but it's great advice for anyone as junior as you are, coming into a job like this."

Google didn't exist then, but with a trip to the library I found an applicable quote attributed to Mark Twain: "It's better to keep your mouth shut and appear stupid than open it and remove all doubt." I subsequently learned that Mark Twain most likely never wrote or said this, but at the time I accepted the premise as holy writ from my new boss-to-be.

The Surgeon General had also received a letter from an influential civilian professor of medicine, Dr. Jay P. Sanford, supporting my assignment to BAMC. Dr. Sanford was a nationally recognized expert in infectious disease and routinely served as a visiting consultant across Army medicine. I had worked with him on several complicated cases at Walter Reed. He was also a close friend and professional colleague of the Army Surgeon General.

Several weeks later, Dr. Sanford was at Walter Reed to consult on several cases. He congratulated me on my upcoming assignment to BAMC, and I took the opportunity to ask him what mistakes I should try to avoid, and how to do that. His immediate response was, "The most common mistake of new junior faculty is to just say out loud whatever comes into their minds at the time, without any consideration of the possible consequences. It's as if their frontal lobes had suddenly atrophied." Then he added, "If they can quickly learn to think before they speak, they can succeed. Otherwise, not."

I arrived at my faculty position at BAMC determined to couple the advice of these two mentors: I would pause before speaking, to give my frontal lobe a little extra time to identify potentially stupid-sounding stuff, and then try to keep the stupid stuff from reaching my vocal cords and passing my lips.

The wisdom of that approach was confirmed when, at my three-month performance review, Dr. Ognibene simply said, "Well, you haven't screwed up in any big way yet. Whatever you're doing seems to be working. Keep it up."

Passing along Dr. Sanford's wise advice, I began to say to residents, "For right now, let's pretend no one heard what you just said. Instead, take some time to carefully run it through your frontal lobe to see if it's still something you want to reach your vocal cords." That year, the annual residents' lampoon show provided an indication that they had heard and processed my message: I was portrayed by an actor wearing a mask with a huge forehead. His only spoken part was to interject, at seemingly random times, "I need a moment to run that through my really big frontal lobe."

Period Two
Don't Get Bitten on the Butt

Towards the end of my time at BAMC, I became fascinated by a newly developing medical specialty, Emergency Medicine (EM), and helped develop the Army's first EM residency at BAMC.

At a national workshop I heard a professor from a civilian emergency medicine residency program say, "In the Emergency Department (ED), errors can easily and quickly bite you and your patients on the butt. I have found my most egregious errors, and their resulting butt-bites, almost always result from forgetting something I already knew: forgetting a fact, forgetting to ask a key question, forgetting to perform an important procedure. Only very rarely do my errors result from not actually knowing something critical to the problem at hand, not knowing about a condition, not knowing the key nature of some clinical element, not knowing how to perform a specific procedure. Thus, my strategy for avoiding butt bite is to constantly struggle to not forget what I already know. That's what I try to teach the residents in our program."

I immediately recognized the validity and the importance of his point. "Don't forget …" became my ED mantra. As I continued working in the BAMC ED, I trained myself to regularly ask, "What am I forgetting?" while examining and treating individual patients. When something went wrong in the care of a patient in our ED, I used the after-action review to search for its root cause. Almost never were knowledge deficits the culprit; almost always the error involved something we should have known, but in the moment forgot.

The most common fear of medical students and residents is that they will hurt a patient because they won't know something important, or won't know how to correctly do something essential. My role became to repeatedly remind them of that professor's wisdom: they must focus on "not forgetting."

Also, the civilian professor's phrase "get bitten on the butt" immediately resonated with me. It was graphic, and the physicians-in-training instantly understood all the things it represented. As residents and students working in the BAMC ED thought and acted their way through clinical scenarios and problems, I regularly reminded them: "Keep asking yourself: 'What will next bite me and my patient on the butt?'" Having appropriated the phrase, I continued to use it in my subsequent teaching.

Period Three
"Good" Decision vs. "Stupid" Decision:
Learning the Difference

Between my assignment to BAMC and when I took command of the West Point hospital, I was assigned as a student at the Army War College to participate in what was essentially a one-year MBA program with a military-specific curriculum.

In a course titled "Combat Commanders Challenge: Decision-Making in a Setting of Incomplete Knowledge," we studied the effects of uncontrollable, seemingly random events—weather, a personal crisis, a change in opposing leadership, etc.—on the consequences of combat leaders' decisions.

In this course, we learned the fallacy of assessing the quality of a combat commander's decision solely on the desirability of the consequences that followed it. In such faulty logic, when those consequences are desirable, the preceding decision must have been good, whereas when those consequences are undesirable, the preceding decision must have been stupid. This common logic error ignores the reality that, based upon only slightly differing (and uncontrollable) circumstances, the same decision can be followed by vastly different consequences, some desirable, and some undesirable.

In fact, as we soon came to understand, the quality of a combat commander's decision should be judged by what its aggregate effect would *likely have been* had that same decision been repeated multiple times in similar circumstances. In this construct:

- "Good" decisions maximize the likelihood that subsequent consequences will, in the aggregate, be desirable. *The occasional occurrence of an undesirable outcome is not proof that the preceding decision was "stupid."*

- "Stupid" decisions maximize the likelihood that subsequent consequences will, in the aggregate, be undesirable. *The occasional occurrence of a desirable outcome is not proof that the preceding decision was "good."*

Re-read these two bullets; they're really important. Judging the value of a decision only by its result is such a common error, and potentially one of great consequence.

Together, these two bullets explain 1) why good decision-making, while usually followed by desired results, does not guarantee such results in each case; and 2) why, occasionally, poor decision-making is followed by a desired result. (Sometimes, stopping at a red light gets you hit from behind and sometimes running a red light is followed by neither accident nor ticket.)

We then studied a variety of decision-support strategies intended to help combat commanders reach decisions that are highly likely to be followed by desirable consequences. These strategies describe how to identify a range of possible decisions, determine the various consequences that could follow each decision, compare the advantages and disadvantages of each of those consequences, and rank the identified possible decisions by their aggregate potential upsides and downsides. For combat commanders, these strategies must sometimes be compressed into a few seconds, such as on a roadside in Iraq when confronting an IED. At other times, they can extend over months, such as in an office in the Pentagon while planning Osama bin Laden's capture.

The take-home message of this course was clear: decisions reached via such decision-support strategies are good decisions, because they increase the likelihood the decision will be followed by desirable consequences. Decisions reached without these considerations are stupid decisions because they increase the likelihood the decision will be followed by undesirable consequences. While this course was intended to teach us how to make good decisions in a combat setting, all the elements could have been found in a similar course for civilian leaders at Harvard Business School.

Period Four
The Stupid Monster Assumes Form

I left West Point for Bethesda, Maryland, to serve as the Commandant of the military's medical school (USU).

Each fall, approximately 170 recent college graduates, newly commissioned as second lieutenants (Army or Air Force) or ensigns (Navy), arrived to start four years of medical studies. Relatively few had any prior military experience.

As Commandant, one of my roles was to deal with infractions of military regulations by these (mostly) new-to-the-military officers. From my prior assignments, I knew that most infractions would be minor, and follow decisions made with little, if any, thought: stupid decisions. Rarely did these students take into consideration that, as military officers, their behaviors would now be judged against standards potentially quite different from those of their recent civilian life. For example, when these new medical students were undergraduates, their Deans were unlikely to have viewed cannabis use as a serious offense; however, as an officer in the US military, testing positive for cannabis on the required random urinalysis—even if it was "just one joint smoked at a concert two weeks ago"—would be a violation of military regulations. Under the Uniformed Code of Military Justice (UCMJ), that violation would be grounds for discharge from their military service and end their enrollment in USU.

Before that year's new USU freshman class was to arrive, I struggled with exactly how to get this message across during my first Commandant's meeting with the class. One evening, while in a movie theater lobby, I saw a poster that provided the visual image I needed:

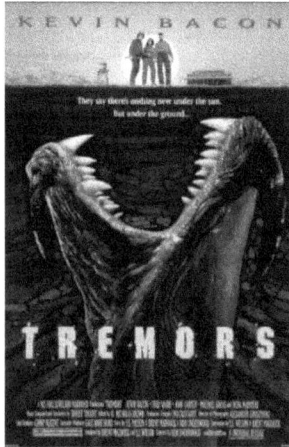

In my subsequent Commandant's meeting, I introduced the new officers to what I termed their "personal Stupid Monsters." I explained that their personal Stupid Monster detects when they were considering doing something stupid, snaps its jaws open awaiting their decision, and if they make the stupid decision, bites them on the butt.

I explained why this was personally important for them: "The only way to avoid the undesirable consequences is to not make the stupid decision in the first place." As an example, I hypothesized two USU students drinking in the same bar. Each drinks the same overly large amount, and each then separately drives home. One makes it home without incident, and the

17

second is stopped and arrested at a random sobriety check. One gets a DUI, gets kicked out of military service, and has to leave this medical school, while the other continues his medical studies. Same stupid decision to drive home, much different consequences.

My central message was, "Before you decide something, ask yourself, 'Did I just hear the sound of my Stupid Monster's jaws snapping open? Is what I'm thinking of doing likely to get me butt-bit?' If your answer is along the lines of 'very likely,' you should consider an alternative, because if you continue along this path, those jaws will most likely clamp shut and you won't control the consequences."

This Stupid Monster construct resonated with the students. I expanded upon it by incorporating the various lessons I'd learned from Drs. Ognibene and Sanford, from the civilian Emergency Medicine professor, from my instructors at the Army War College, and from my time in command of the West Point hospital.

During my four years as USU Commandant, I routinely employed an expanded Stupid Monster analogy in a series of Commandant's meetings with the school's officer-students where we discussed issues of officership and leadership they would face following their graduation. During those discussions I realized that awareness of the Stupid Monster, before it actually butt-bit, could provide warning that the decision under consideration would benefit from additional thought. Developing and nurturing such awareness could shape-shift a Stupid Monster into a guard dog with a useful warning bark.

Thus were born what the members of a series of USU medical student classes have called "Colonel Wolcott's Stupid Monster Talks," which went on to form the basis for this book.

The next chapter will introduce you to the star of this book: your Stupid Monster.

CHAPTER TWO
MEET YOUR STUPID MONSTER

I describe the Stupid Monster as a *graboid* similar to its cousins in the movie series *Tremors* with Kevin Bacon. We each have one, and it:

- Pays attention to our decision-making
- Snaps open its jaws whenever it detects we are contemplating a stupid decision
- Delivers a *Tremors*-like bite on the butt if we actually make that stupid decision

Since stupid decisions are frequently followed by undesirable consequences, the snapping open of the Stupid Monster's jaws is a harbinger of undesirable consequences likely to follow. (In Chapter 3 you will learn how to detect that opening snap—to figuratively "hear the jaws snap open.")

The following examples showcase three historically stupid decisions, their resultant pre-butt-bite jaw-opening, and the extremely undesirable consequences that followed.

The Stupid Monster in the Garden of Eden

Adam and Eve were pleasantly lounging about in the Garden of Eden. God told them that they could do anything they wanted to do in that Garden, except for one thing. Eve suggested, "Despite what God said, don't you think we could follow that serpent's advice and eat some of this lovely forbidden fruit?" *Opening snap*! As each ate of the tree's fruit, an open-jawed Stupid Monster prepared to bite their butts.

Their stupid decision was followed by God's eternal curses upon each of the three participants and their progeny: men, to a lifetime of hard labor followed by death; women, to the pain of childbirth and subordination to their husbands; and serpents, to crawl on their bellies while suffering the enmity of both men and women.

The wages of stupid don't get any larger than that!

The Stupid Monster in the Dakota Territory

On June 25, 1876, General George Custer decided that he would personally lead one-third of the roughly 600 officers and enlisted members of his command, the 7th Cavalry, in a mid-day attack on a Native American encampment along the Little Big Horn River in what is today North Dakota. His decision rested on a series of fallacious assumptions: that his force would face no more than 800 hostiles; that they would be unaware of his approach; that when he attacked, they would be in their encampment along a riverbank; and that his troops were far superior fighters to those he would face. Custer chose not to conduct a reconnaissance to determine the area's precise topography or the actual size and location of the opposing force . . . *opening snap!* In fact, that day he and his troopers would face many thousands of North America's finest warriors who were well aware of his presence and were deploying to confront him. Off he rode as his Stupid Monster delivered a butt-bite, which his foes soon followed with a scalping!

(Note: I feel a very personal attachment to this engagement. My great-grandfather, a Civil War veteran, had rejoined the Army and been assigned to the 7th Cavalry some months earlier, but was not with Custer's troops that day. Instead, he was confined in an Army stockade, having been arrested shortly after having deserted. As he recounted in a letter to his wife back in Massachusetts, "I worry Custer's glory hunting is going to get everyone killed; I'm going to run; even if I get caught, I'd rather be in the stockade." To my mind, this was a common soldier's very astute analysis of the possible upside and possible downside risks associated with a decision's consequences.)

A Stupid Monster Attack in Germany

On May 6, 1937, the German passenger airship LZ 129 Hindenburg sailed through a spring thunderstorm and approached its mooring mast at the Lakehurst Naval Air Station. The airship, completing a transatlantic voyage, carried 36 passengers and 61 crewmen. Its owners had decided to fill this commercial airship with highly flammable hydrogen gas rather than non-flammable helium gas. They based their decision upon a combination of economic factors (hydrogen was far less expensive than was helium); political factors (while Nazi Germany could produce hydrogen, the United States controlled all sources of helium); and engineering factors (their engineers repeatedly assured them that the Hindenburg's design, construction, and operation "totally removed the risk of fire"). Unfortunately, the owners did not give appropriate weight to the various downside risks of fire. *Opening snap!* The airship went into commercial service, and the jaws of the owners' Stupid Monsters closed shut. The subsequent hydrogen-fed fire burned though the airship in seconds. Thirty-six people died, and newsreel footage showing the disaster in real time was viewed by millions of moviegoers around the world. Deutsche Zeppelin-Reederi, the German parent company, declared bankruptcy.

While it is the seriousness of their consequences that makes each of these three examples so memorable, what makes them important to readers of this book is their common underlying cause: each resulted from a stupid decision. Just think how different the results might have been had Adam, Custer, and the

Hindenburg's owners detected the opening snap of the jaws of their personal Stupid Monsters, and thus avoided the stupid decisions for which they are now remembered. What if:

- Adam had urged, "Look. Let's give this some thought. I really worry that nothing good can come from angering the God who created all this."
- Custer had reasoned, "I don't want to accidentally ride into a trap; I'd best send out a reconnaissance party."
- The Hindenburg's owners had decided, "You know, we can't afford to expose our customers, our company, or the Reich to even the small risk of a catastrophic fire; use the helium, instead."

The next chapter of this book will teach you how to detect that opening snap, and how to treat that detection as a warning that a better decision is needed if you wish to avoid a butt-bite and its associated undesired consequences.

TO IMPROVE NOW

In the space provided here, write down what you consider the three most stupid decision you have made in the past two years and their consequences.

Decision	Consequences

Considering the decisions above, how might the consequences have been different had you made an alternative decision?

Alternative Decision	Consequences

Later in this book, you'll be asked to return and re-examine these decisions to see how effective your new skill set—acquired by reading and studying this book—would have been in alerting you before you made these stupid decisions, and in helping you to identify, evaluate and select alternatives with their different) consequences.

PART TWO

TAMING YOUR STUPID MONSTER

For most people, the Stupid Monster will always remain a dangerous wild animal lurking just out of view and biding its time before butt-biting, like a wild wolf in the forest around an arctic cabin.

However, by following the lessons of this book, you will develop the skills to shape-shift your Stupid Monster from a wild animal, whose attack you fear but cannot predict, into a watch dog you trained to bark when you are considering potentially stupid decisions— whenever the jaws of your Stupid Monster have snapped open. When recognized and heeded, these "warning barks" will alert you to an impending stupid decision, providing time for you to weigh alternative decisions and to avoid (or at least to mitigate) the consequences of choosing stupidly.

The central message of *Taming Your Stupid Monster* is that you can master these skills and routinely put them into practice. They fall into the following categories:

- Detecting and being warned by the opening snap (aka, recognizing the warning bark)
- Dealing with factors that can impair your detection of that opening snap
- Responding effectively when warned

CHAPTER THREE

DETECTING THE OPENING SNAP

Poker players call the subconscious physical responses that occur in certain table situations "tells." Excellent poker players identify their opponents' tells in order to spot a strong, or a weak, opposing hand. They also work to suppress their own tells in order to deny their opponents a similar advantage. Poker players who never learn to recognize and deal with tells are known for their really poor poker play.

In a similar manner, we each have our unique response (or responses) to the opening snap of our Stupid Monster's jaws; those responses are our personal pre-stupidity tells. People who never learn to recognize and deal with their pre-stupidity tells are known for their really stupid decisions.

I have come to recognize that, in different circumstances, I exhibit different tells in response to an opening jaw snap. I work to recognize each response as a pre-stupidity warning. Each is, in fact, a bark of my guard dog. Mine are:

- *A cold ball suddenly appearing at the bottom of my stomach*: This tell occurs most often in settings where I am making a (potentially stupid) decision involving some physical danger, whether to myself or to others; examples include driving in heavy traffic, trying to land a small plane in a crosswind, and teaching a grandchild to ride a bike.
- *A startle sensation*: This tell makes me feel as if I need to catch my balance after stepping into an unexpected hole or encountering an extra stairstep. It occurs most often when I have just begun to act on a (potentially stupid) decision.
- *A feeling like seeing something bad in my peripheral vision:* This tell duplicates the sensation triggered by something (car, bike, motorcycle) suddenly running the light while I'm in a crosswalk. This is the tell I most commonly experience when considering a (potentially) stupid decision in my day-to-day life.

I am certain that a clinical psychologist would find that my tells have deep-rooted psychological origins, and that yours likely would have, as well. However, the psychological origins of your tells are unimportant to taming your Stupid Monster. What is important is that you learn to recognize each of your tells and accept them as your unique warning system—the bark of your personal guard dog—alerting you that the Stupid Monster, with jaws newly snapped open, is nearby.

Once you can reliably identify your personal tells, you will have begun the conversion of your wild Stupid Monster into your watch dog. Try this to help identify your personal pre-stupidity tell:

TO IMPROVE NOW

Imagine you are in your car driving down a moderately busy two-lane town street, the green traffic light three car lengths ahead of you changes to yellow, and your immediate impulse is to run through it.

Even as your gas pedal foot prepares to stomp down, you would likely experience at least a microsecond of indecision and feel something. What would that feeling be? Would it be sweaty palms, a tingling in the back of your neck, a tightness in your chest, nausea, or even itchy feet?

Whatever the feeling, it's important that you identify and remember it. That feeling is probably a personal pre-stupidity tell. Recognize its presence as a warning bark that the Stupid Monster is nearby with open jaws, and that a butt-bite threatens. Whenever you experience this feeling in the future—however weakly or strongly—pause, be so warned, and strongly consider implementing alternative decisions.

TO IMPROVE LATER

Each day for the next week, as you are about to make an everyday decision, pause to deliberately ask yourself, "Does anything about how I'm feeling suggest the nearness of the Stupid Monster?" (These decisions can be as simple as selecting a menu option in a restaurant or as complicated as choosing how to respond to a co-worker's criticism. What is important is searching your gut for a tell that suggests the Stupid Monster's jaws have snapped and your guard dog has barked.)

Make a written record of potential personal tells. Your personal warning system may, as does mine, have more than one way to alert you. Also note the situation in which you recognized the tell.

Situation	Possible Tell

Summary

Developing sufficient awareness to recognize your own tells is essential to successfully taming your Stupid Monster. Alerted by your tells, you gain the time to proactively consider alternative decisions; unalerted, you will forever be simply reacting to the unanticipated butt-bites and undesirable consequences that follow your stupid decisions.

Identifying your tells is not sufficient to tame your Stupid Monster. Multiple factors can blunt your awareness of them, impairing your ability to recognize and effectively heed the warning bark. Chapter Four discusses the most common reasons such warnings pass unheeded and provides suggestions to avoid or counter them.

CHAPTER FOUR

DON'T LET THE WARNING GO UNHEEDED

Certain situations and aspects of your personality can make it difficult to hear the warning bark or recognize a tell. Because this is true for nearly everyone, in this chapter I provide descriptions, examples, and defenses against each of the most common factors to help you determine which are most likely to affect you and to then strengthen your defenses accordingly.

Personality Traits

Personality is relatively fixed over time; so too are its effects on decision-making. Individuals exhibiting certain personality traits are particularly prone to routinely reaching poorly thought-through decisions. The three personality traits described here might describe you normally, or perhaps they appear only under certain circumstances. Might you exhibit one or more of these? If so, this accentuates the importance of recognizing your tell and of heeding the warning.

The impulsive/impetuous routinely select either the first decision that occurs to them or the decision that is immediately appealing, and usually based upon the most superficial of reasons. They often misperceive (and later defend) their impulsive actions as having been decisive, but truly decisive people have analyzed their options and made a decision within applicable time constraints. Impulsive people frequently blame any undesirable consequences of their decisions on bad luck.

The phrase "impulsiveness of youth" is a cliché, but it does reflect basic development patterns within the human brain. Until approximately age 25, the connections between the frontal lobes and the limbic system of the brain—the parts that allow exercise of control over impulsive behavior and allow evaluation of comparative risks—are still evolving. People under age 25 are predisposed to act impulsively; some retain this behavior later into their lives. Examples:

- Adam and Eve certainly exemplified the adverse effects that impulsiveness can exert over decision-making.
- I tend to respond impulsively to email criticisms and complaints; early on, I reflexively sent poorly considered (angry) responses, which often created problems. My solution was to

create a "delay send" function within my email account. When clicked, my email was diverted to a holding file for my later review. It would stay there until I deleted it, deliberately sent it, or revised it and sent the revision. As a result, I sent far fewer poorly considered responses and spent far less time repairing the resulting damage.

- *Case Study 1 (The Lawn Worker)* (page 75) is an example of how my own impulsive behavior earned me a butt-bite.

Arrogance can be hard to detect or acknowledge within yourself, but it is an important factor to consider. The arrogant assume their decisions will always be correct and move forward on that basis, neither validating their assumptions, consulting expert sources, nor seeking advice from friends or colleagues. These people frequently attribute any unwanted consequences of their decisions to "someone else's mistake." The Greek word *hubris* (meaning pridefulness, self-importance, or self-conceit) is essentially interchangeable with arrogance. Examples:

- By all contemporary accounts, General Custer was arrogance personified, and his decisions along the Little Big Horn River are consistent with that behavior trait.

- I find arrogance to more commonly afflict decisions I make in my personal life, rather than those I face in my medical or leadership roles. I have to be particularly aware of this when personal life decisions involve money. I was brought up viewing money decisions as being in the domain of the man of the house. Thus, I entered my married life making those decisions unilaterally. Many butt-bites later I recognized the underlying arrogance of my belief and changed the decision-making process regarding what I then understood as our money.

- *Case Study 2 (Pushball Pushes Back)* (page 81) incidentally demonstrates how an officer's repeated arrogant decision-making effectively ended his military career . . . even without getting soldiers killed along the Little Big Horn River.

Those who can be **intellectually dishonest** or **lack moral courage** base their decisions on a distortion of reality reflecting their biases and prejudices. These people either cannot see or simply deny that their biased, prejudiced, or personal risk-averse decisions were the trigger for any unwanted consequences. Examples:

- The Hindenburg's owners displayed their intellectual dishonesty both by initially bowing to Nazi pressure to build a 100% German airship, and later by attributing the disaster to sabotage.

- I arrived at USU as Commandant having been "successful" for several years as a senior medical office in the Army. Accustomed to (and comfortable with) the Army way of doing things, I was generally dismissive of any need for USU to operate parallel Navy or Air Force policies and procedures. However, since the staff and students at USU came from all three services, my early, narrow-minded, one-size-fits-all decisions quickly caused a wide variety of problems for the school's Navy and Air Force service members. After a decision I made caused several Navy and Air Force officers to be incorrectly paid by their services, the medical school dean, Dr. Sanford, told me, "Barry, I didn't bring you here to straighten out the Navy or Air Force, no matter how much better you think the Army does something. Your job here is to make things work easily, and for everyone, regardless of their service."

- *Case Study 14 (Wisdom Teeth Wisdom)* (page 151) presents a senior surgeon who was unwilling to acknowledge that his reasons for objecting to a policy change were a professional prejudice he held regarding dentists.

TO IMPROVE NOW

Of the personality traits discussed above, identify the one that contributes most often to your decisions with undesired consequences. As illustrated in the arrogance example, a trait might affect you in certain areas but not others. If they could answer anonymously, what would your family or colleagues say? _____

TO IMPROVE LATER

If impulsiveness, arrogance, or intellectual dishonesty appear (to you and/or to your colleagues or family) to regularly drive your decision-making, you might seriously consider accompanying the various lessons in this book with professional outside help to ameliorate those traits. With or without such outside help, it will be beneficial for you to be aware that your decision-making appears (to yourself or to others) to be influenced by these traits, and that as a result you are particularly susceptible to making stupid decisions. To defend against the deleterious effect of these traits, you must continually be hyper-alert to your tells and hyper-vigilant in treating them as true warnings, and continually act deliberately to avoid the stupid decisions they facilitate. Like a watchmaker with poor vision who must always wear his glasses, I still keep over my workplace, for easy and regular review, a small framed card saying "Beware of Impulsivity."

Behaviors

Many behaviors transiently alter your brain's decision-making processes—almost never a good thing. Some lower your inhibitions, thus increasing impulsiveness; some impair your ability to weigh consequences; and many do both. These alterations increase the chances of reaching a decision with unanticipated bad consequences, making it easier to do stupid.

Drugs and **alcohol** exert their effects by both blunting your ability to accurately evaluate the risks/benefits of possible decisions, and by increasing impulsiveness by blunting normal inhibitions. Examples:

- During my year at the Army War College, a senior infantry officer provided me with sage advice about avoiding the deleterious effects of drinking on decision-making: "Drinking in private may cause problems in your personal life; I can't help you deal with those. However, drinking in social settings easily leads to professional problems. Accept that any drinking impairs your judgment and act to minimize that impairment." Below are the rules he espoused

to GOVERN HIS SOCIAL DRINKING:

- Never have more than two alcoholic drinks at any public event.
- Always have an appropriate drink glass in your hand so no one can easily force another one on you.
- Bribe the bartender at the start of the evening to always make "your special drink" that contains no (or almost no) alcohol. You can tell a person who insists on buying you a drink to "see George at the bar; he knows just how I like it."
- Avoid making business decisions in such settings. Learn to say something like, "That's well worth discussing; call me, and we'll be able to give it the time it deserves." (Early on as a physician, I was plagued by people at parties asking me about their medical issues. I finally learned to say, "No problem. Just go over to that chair, take off your clothes, and I'll examine you properly . . . or, if you prefer, call and make an appointment to see me at my office.")
- *Case Study 5 (Happy Birthday: The Crime)* (page 99) is an example of how the lowered inhibitions from what started as "innocent drinking" by three soldiers led to a series of

stupid decisions followed by potentially life-altering consequences.

High emotions, like anger, grief, passion, fear, and their close relatives, can focus your attention on some decision options while minimizing attention to others. Being angry, depressed, set on having revenge, or desperately trying to impress yourself or others increases the chance you will fail to detect or heed a warning of potential stupidity. Examples:

- The driver in the Subaru had used the access road shoulder to bypass the long line of cars crawling along to enter the thruway. When he was aggressively trying to squeeze in front of me as the shoulder ran out, I was so furious at his "road hog" attitude that I was about to risk a collision by not letting him in. My grandson's comment, "Grandpa, isn't he being stupid!" served as my watchdog bark. The Subaru driver was *being* stupid, but I had been about to *do* stupid; when making decisions in traffic, as with most things in life, two stupids do not make a smart.

- *Case Study 4 (Diamonds are Forever)* (page 93) is an example of a happier emotion leading to doing stupid. Lieutenant Lafferty was so thrilled by having become engaged earlier that day that she failed to detect her guard dog's bark trying

41

to warn her that telling her commanding officer of her engagement to a West Point cadet (a huge no-no) would lead directly to a butt-bite.

Distraction and **inattention** reduce the effort available for analyzing the relative merits of possible decisions, thus increasing the likelihood that the decision made will be less than the best. Call it multi-tasking, juggling too many balls at the same time, or just having too much to do at the moment, you are much more likely to miss the alarm and face the consequences of the resulting stupid decision. Example:

- I was focused on trying to get a large caliber intravenous line started in the patient on exam table #4. He had thrown up a whole lot of bright red blood just after arriving at the Emergency Department (ED) complaining of stomach pains. I heard the nurse behind me say, "Doctor Wolcott, I'm putting an asthma patient in table #1," as she wheeled another patient into the evaluation area, but I didn't look up. I was "distracted." Fortunately for the patient, the nurse then said, very emphatically, "Dr. Wolcott. This patient needs you right now!" When I looked over to exam table #1, I saw that the patient's lips and skin were dark blue and that she was not breathing. I had been so focused on my task at hand that I had ignored my watchdog's barked warning: "In the ED, always look closely at every new patient to be certain they aren't sicker than the patient you're currently evaluating."

Bravado, or **showing-off**—whether to yourself, your friends or family, your peers or subordinates, or your boss—can make poor decisions more likely.

- "Barry," said the Assistant Athletic Director in the midst of the controlled chaos that always accompanied the yearly arrival and in-processing of 1,200 new cadet candidates to West Point, "I need you to work your magic. One of our best lacrosse recruits busted his upper arm a couple of days ago. He's doing fine, but it's in a cast. I told Coach Jackson here that all he needs is for you to sign off on a waiver and the recruit can be sworn in—that as Hospital Commander, you have the authority to do that." He handed me the paperwork. The lacrosse coach smiled and said, "Must be nice to have magical powers."

  The appeals to my ego worked; I signed.

  A few minutes later, I realized that I had been so busy showing off that I had not heard my guard dog's bark. I should have had the cadet candidate evaluated by the orthopedic staff before I made any decision regarding a waiver.

43

That bad decision resulted in my having to quickly eat two bowls of crow: one when I had to tell the coach that, despite my having signed the paperwork, his player still needed to see the orthopedists; and the second when I told the orthopedists that I had inappropriately undercut their role in the waiver process. The good news was that the cadet candidate still received a waiver, but properly based upon the orthopedists' recommendations.

- *Case Study 3 (Toboggan or Not To-boggan)* (page 88) is an example of how a normally smart officer and physician got caught up in showing off to himself, ignored the warning bark of his guard dog, and ended up in the ED as a result.

Defending against the effects of such behaviors requires openly acknowledging their potential for facilitating stupid decisions, identifying when one of the behaviors is actively affecting you, and deliberately avoiding making a decision until the impairing effect has worn off. Rather than rushing ahead—despite warnings (and perhaps even a recognition) that your decision-making is transiently impaired—it is almost always better to delay making a decision in such settings. It rarely takes very long for your temper to come back under control, for the urge to show off to fade, or for two strong coffees and a few minutes to reduce your alcohol impairment. I learned to explain to my subordinates that when I was angry, I frequently made less than optimal decisions and asked that they warn me when I seemed to be making decisions in that state. We agreed that they could simply say, "Temper, boss! Temper!" and I would re-examine my decision.

TO IMPROVE NOW

Consider the behaviors discussed above: drugs and alcohol, high emotions, distraction or inattention, and bravado. Identify two that you feel contribute most often to decisions with undesired consequences. If they could answer anonymously, what would your family or colleagues   say?

_____

TO IMPROVE LATER

To help you get a sense of how often these behaviors appeared in your life over the past month, use the table below to track those you considered above, along with a note about the decision you made, and your evaluation of it.

Behavior	Decision	Evaluation of the decision

Specific Settings

The setting in which we consider a decision affects the decision process we employ. Each of the settings I discuss below puts you at a high risk of blunting your ability to heed the warning offered by the opening snap of the Stupid Monster's jaws; this is certainly true for me. By recognizing that you are making a decision in such elevated risk situations, you can effectively deal with that risk by increasing your focus on employing high-quality decision-making. When you find yourself in one of these situations, listen extra hard for the warning bark.

High profile/High visibility settings: For actors on the stage, being in the spotlight brings out their best; that is rarely the case for the rest of us. Whether it's the spotlight of the media, of public opinion, or of peers, this situation easily interferes with structured decision-making, thus rendering butt-bites more likely. Your visibility is dramatically increased in today's high-intensity social media and video-rich environments. (Considering a rapid response to a tweet or a blog post? Remember how many people might actually see it . . . now and later.)

- Three patients alleged that a member of the West Point hospital staff had acted inappropriately while caring for them, and the newspapers and TV news were reporting on the situation. Our formal investigation of these allegations was not yet complete. Unfortunately, when a TV reporter shoved a microphone in my face and asked, "Colonel Wolcott, what have you decided to do about this?" my unprepared response and mannerisms made it sound as if the investigation was inappropriately biased in favor of the staff member. Stupidly, and disconcerted by the cluster of reporters and cameras, I spoke without having thought through what I would say and how I would present myself. The high-visibility setting had muffled the warning bark of my guard dog.

"Just a second"/"One last thing" situations: I have learned to treat the use of such phrases as an attempt by the speaker to blunt my awareness of my guard dog's warning bark. Each phrase is meant by the speaker to imply that the issue that follows is trivial; in my experience, it almost never is.

Experience has also taught me the wisdom of being extra careful when additional high-risk phrases follow the initial "Just one more thing …" statement made as a meeting is ending. These include:

- "I need you to do something for me ..."
- "Can you please fix this ..."
- "I know you can make this go away ..."
- "I need a personal favor ..."
- "I'd be really grateful if you could ..."
- "Normally, I wouldn't ask, but ..."

These phrases are common preludes to requests I later find either mired in office politics, of questionable ethical merit, or possibly illegal.

A different but closely related phrase is "Can I tell you something in confidence?" Asking for permission to reveal a confidence is more common in settings where the speaker is the less powerful participant. This phrase is generally spoken in the hope of generating a reflexive response from you—to get you to agree to hear an otherwise undescribed issue while also agreeing in advance to do so in confidence.

It's easy to feel flattered when someone is willing to share a confidence. Reflexively replying with something like *sure*, or *no problem*, or *go ahead* is easy to do when you anticipate nothing more than some minor item of gossip. However, unless you are the person's spouse, lawyer, or clergyman, entering into a confidentiality agreement that is simultaneously undefined and open-ended causes the Stupid Monster's jaws to snap open

- *Case Study 7 (Before You Go)* (page 110) discusses a number of issues potentially arising in such settings

New-to-us or **unexpected events:** As we gain experience successfully making decisions, we face fewer and fewer issues we haven't faced before, or issues arising outside their usual settings. As a result, most issues look pretty close to something we are used to dealing with. In such cases, there is a strong temptation to take an intellectual shortcut and simply apply a decision that worked pretty well before without considering that this particular case is different in some important way, and thus merits additional consideration. Taking the shortcut muffles the warning bark and frequently leads to butt-bite.

- Early in my medical residency at Walter Reed, a woman in her 70s was admitted to the Medical Intensive Care Unit (ICU) where I was the on-duty physician. The paramedics said she had a stroke at a local shopping mall. An ID card showed her daughter was an Army officer stationed in a nearby city. I found the woman's speech to be totally garbled, but that she had no paralysis. In those days before CAT scans and clot busters, there was little to do but provide supportive care. Seeing nothing unusual in the patient's findings, I simply awaited her daughter's arrival. When she arrived a few hours later, I learned that the patient's speech was actually quite clear—to the bilingual daughter—and that her Bulgarian-speaking mother had simply tripped and fallen while shopping. Apparently everyone, including me, had assumed what was actually clear Bulgarian was, instead, English garbled by a stroke. I had taken an intellectual shortcut and accepted the paramedics' field assessment as fact.

- The sergeant in *Case Study 9* (*Pizza Party*) (page 121) was experienced in the use of Army ambulances, but in an unusual-for-her setting failed to distinguish a legitimate ambulance use from a non-legitimate one because "at the time, it didn't seem like much of a difference."

Role ambiguity or unclarity: Over the course of a day, we each assume various roles within the ongoing drama that is our life. At one moment we are a customer in a store; at another, we are a student in a classroom; at yet another we are a worker speaking to our supervisor. Usually we move seamlessly between our roles without thought, adopting role-appropriate behaviors, speech, and sometimes costumes. When those with whom we are interacting recognize our current role and we recognize theirs, the drama goes on as expected.

Over the course of my several careers, I have learned that the risks of stupid increase a great deal in situations where individuals' roles are misidentified. Today, I work aggressively and proactively to ensure that everyone involved agrees about the roles appropriate to the situation at hand. I do so to avoid the stupid consequences that easily and frequently follow role ambiguity.

In the workplace, I am frequently very blunt about this. I routinely make the following statements to new employees:

1. I am capable of interacting with you in several different roles: as supervisor, as colleague, as mentor, or as friend. If I am ever acting in a role other than as supervisor, I will always try to let you know. If during an interaction, I need to change roles, I will try to let you know that as well. If you would like me to assume a role other than supervisor for a specific interaction with you, please tell me so. I will tell you if I can support that.

2. You are capable of interacting with me in several different roles: as subordinate, as colleague, as mentee, or as friend. Unless you tell me differently, when we are in the workplace I will interact with you assuming you are in the role of employee. Please let me know if, during any specific interaction, you would like to assume a

different role; I will tell you if I can support that."

While at first such an approach sounds a bit schizophrenic, I have found it a highly efficient mechanism to increase effective dialogue among members of a group.

Unicorns: When people suddenly find themselves in a situation "not dreamt of in [their] philosophy"—a unicorn situation—they often fail to hear the warning bark. Instead of carefully thinking things through, they often respond impulsively with reflex decisions relatively uninhibited by any frontal lobe consideration. Butt-bite is a frequent result.

- *Case Study 8 (Deer in the Pool)* (page 116) shows how one decision maker responded poorly when confronting what was to him a unicorn: a deer in an indoor Olympic-sized swimming pool!

Policies/Rules/Regulations: While these are created to encourage making the correct decisions, and to ensure uniformity of decisions across time and space, they should remain merely tools. Slavish reliance on them as a replacement for thinking things through is an invitation to a butt-bite and its consequences. Any time the best justification you can give for a decision is simply that it is required by rules, regulations, or policies, a butt-bite and its consequences are soon to follow.

- *Case Study 11 (Too Much of a Surgeon)* (page 131) displays how a rational decision replaced an earlier stupid decision that slavishly followed the letter of a regulation.

TO IMPROVE NOW

Consider the settings discussed above: high profile/high visibility; "just a second"/"one last thing"; new or unexpected events; role ambiguity or unclarity; unicorns; and policies, rules, and regulations. Identify the two that most often contribute to decisions with undesired consequences. If they could answer anonymously, what would your family or colleagues say? _____

TO IMPROVE LATER

We all have factors that can interfere with our ability to hear the barking of our guard dog; developing awareness of our personal areas of greatest "hearing loss" is an important skill. I have recorded below those that are most problematic to me:

	Barry's Most Problematic Area for Decision-Making
Personality Trait:	Impulsivity

| Behavior: | Emotion (Anger) |
| Setting: | One last thing |

For this exercise, pull together what you have considered and learned about the factors that can negatively influence your personal ability to make a good decision and record them here:

	Most Problematic Area for Decision-Making
Personality Trait:	
Behavior:	
Setting:	

Chapter Summary

The ability to recognize your personal tells is central to eventually taming your Stupid Monster, but knowledge of them alone might fail to protect you from butt-bite. Only a *recognized* bark can provide you with an opportunity for improved decision-making. Making use of this opportunity requires an understanding of and defense against specific traits, behaviors, and settings that can impair your ability to first detect and then act in response to warning barks.

The next chapter deals with making effective use of the opportunity your new skills provide. Before proceeding, be confident that you have identified your own pre-stupidity tells and know how to deal effectively with the personal traits, behaviors, and settings that affect your ability to hear the warning barks resulting from recognition of those tells. If you feel less than fully confident, time spent reviewing the applicable portions of Chapters Three and Four will be well-invested.

CHAPTER FIVE

EFFECTIVELY HEEDING
THE WARNING

Recognizing when an opening jaw-snap has triggered the bark of your personal pre-stupidity warning is an acquired skill; you began practicing it in Chapter Three. In Chapter Four you looked inward to detect attributes, behaviors, and situations that interfere with your recognizing that alarm, and learned proactive measures to avoid such interference.

With these skills and personal knowledge in hand, successfully taming your Stupid Monster requires you to actually make informed use of that warning. Making informed use requires you to adopt and adhere to an intellectual discipline that identifies and analyzes alternative decisions and then guides you to deliberately avoid those that are stupid.

Adopting and adhering to any new discipline can be presented as a complex and lengthy process; the scope of effective decision-making is deep and wide, with books, articles, podcasts, and lengthy academic courses.

However, I have written this chapter as an easy-to-use primer. The techniques are effective for everyday use, and are intentionally not an in-depth exposition on decision analysis. I based this chapter on simple techniques I have learned during my career-long journey with stupid, and provide the case studies in Part Three as additional examples of various practical decision-analysis techniques for your study and consideration.

Let me pause here to emphasize again that the techniques of this easy-to-use decision-analysis primer will *only* be valuable to you if you can successfully identify that you are about to make a potentially stupid decision. If you are aware of your tells, treat them as warning barks, and overcome your personal impairments to hearing those barks, you will enjoy the opportunity to identify, evaluate, and select from alternative decisions.

My decision-making lessons fall into five general categories:

- There is almost always time to think
- You can avoid paralysis-by-analysis
- Consequences count
- Two heads are (usually) better than one
- Consider using an abbreviated decision analysis methodology

There is almost always time to think. Very few decisions actually need to be made reflexively; rare exceptions would include braking for suddenly-appearing baby carriages, avoiding falling pianos, and ducking when being shot at. (In fact, wondering if you have time to think usually means you **do** have that time, otherwise you would have already acted reflexively.) Experience has taught me to treat the thought *there isn't time to think about it* as a tell.

As described on page 11, poor decisions in the Emergency Department (ED) result more frequently from forgetting something we already know than from not knowing something we should have known. My experience is that this is equally true outside the ED, and outside of medicine entirely. Taking time to think and to ask, "what am I forgetting?" allows for important remembering, regardless of your context.

One Saturday I was called to the West Point hospital's ED because "we've got sick cadets all over the place." When I arrived, there were about 25 cadets in various stages of nausea, vomiting, and diarrhea filling the ED and forming a squalid line at its doors; pretty clearly, we were facing the first cases of an outbreak of something. The odds were good that where there were 25 now, there would very quickly be a lot more. The ED staff wanted to get the cadets already on-scene quickly admitted to the hospital to clear space for the anticipated new arrivals. Our small hospital seemed to be facing an emergency, and seemed soon to be overwhelmed with far more patients than it could handle. The ED physician was calling for action "right now."

The senior sergeant working in the ED pulled me aside and said, "Sir. This is a huge mess, but it's really not an emergency; no one is dying. There are already too many to simply admit them routinely; there wouldn't even be enough regular beds, to say nothing of all the regular paperwork for each admission. Let me deal with what's here as best as I can. That will let you and the staff figure out how to deal with what may well turn out to be several hundred sick cadets."

After about 45 minutes, we had worked out a plan: we placed 200 stretchers in the corridors and provided each with bedding, bedpans, vomit-buckets, and intravenous supplies; truncated the required admission paperwork; maintained an accurate roster of all the admitted patients; and called in off-duty staff to care for the expected load of patients. It worked. Over the next three to four days we admitted and discharged several hundred cadets without incident. The sergeant had recognized what neither the ED physician nor I had: there really was time to think!

Yes, the amount of time spent thinking about a decision must be appropriate to the situation and to the potential consequences; it may be very time-constrained or quite lengthy (page 15). However, failing to think (or

59

its cousin "not thinking long enough") is a far more common problem than is spending too much time contemplating a decision.

TO IMPROVE NOW

Recall the last time you felt pressured to make a decision. Did the pressure come from the outside (a boss or a significant other pressing for immediate action), or was it self-imposed (perhaps you wanted to appear decisive (page 34))? What could you have done or said to buy yourself some time to think? In my office, I actually took to keeping a one-minute sand glass on my desk and when contemplating a rush decision, saying to myself, "There's always time to think." Outside my office I took to saying out loud, "I have learned through experience that there's almost always time to think. Give me a minute to do just that."

TO IMPROVE LATER

Identify a particular setting (personal or professional) in which you are likely to be *repeatedly* pressured to make too-quick decisions. Write down— and practice saying out loud—a response designed to gain you the time you need without creating animosity. (In such situations, a colleague of mine was fond of saying, "I can give you the right decision or I can give you a decision right now. You can't have both. Which do you want?") Over the next month, put this into practice whenever possible as a way to ingrain the approach.

You can avoid paralysis-by-analysis. Clearly, no one's days are long enough to subject every decision to the full-analysis process taught in business schools. I have found these techniques generally unhelpful in my everyday personal and business life because of the extreme difficulty of identifying all possible consequences and agreeing on the value of each consequence. You need a fast-track process to screen the myriad of decisions you make every day—those decisions that "don't seem all that important" and that, therefore, you are tempted to make reflexively. Here is my minimalist approach for such situations:

1. Ask and answer the question I suggested the USU medical students employ (page 18): "Did I just hear the sound of my Stupid Monster's jaws snapping open? Is what I'm thinking of doing likely to get me butt-bit?" Usually the answer will be no, and you can quickly move on. (Note that this approach depends upon a well-developed ability to recognize your tell and successfully adapting to any traits, behaviors, or special situations that would blunt that recognition.)

2. If the answer to this screening question is yes, asking follow-on questions may well help

explain why your pre-stupidity warning was triggered and assist in identifying whether you will be best served by considering alternative decisions. Ask yourself the following additional questions:

- Is it ethical?
- Is it legal?
- Is it *not* self-serving?
- Is it *not* ego-driven?
- Would it please my mother/boss/mentor?
- Would I be proud to read it on the front page of the newspaper, in my obituary, or on my tombstone?

If the answer to any one of these questions is no, I recommend pausing, taking a deep breath, and considering that this decision probably deserves more consideration than you initially allocated to it.

If you answer yes to each question, this generally indicates that the warning was a false alarm that you can safely ignore. However, as a further check I frequently add the question, "Can I live with the worst thing that is likely to happen as a result of this decision?" Answering no to this question also indicates that the decision requires more consideration than initially allocated.

TO IMPROVE NOW

Identify five recent decisions that, in retrospect, you now consider as having been stupid. For each decision, think about the sequence of screening (and follow-up) questions and indicate which decisions would have benefitted from this approach.

Decision	Did you detect the opening snap?	Would the screening questions have helped you to detect it?

If taking the extra time to ask those questions in the five decisions you made (or even just one or two of them) would have been worth your while, what can you do to remind yourself to ask them when you make future decisions? If not, can you imagine a decision you are likely to face that would so benefit?

Consequences count. A common decision-making error is to act as if only a single consequence can follow a contemplated decision. That is rarely the case. In fact, several different consequences are generally possible.

Each potential consequence has its own unique likelihood of actually occurring, and that's why making the decision does not guarantee which specific one of those consequences will follow.

Also, as described in the Case Study 9 "*Pizza Party*" (page 121) individual consequences may have both desired attributes (the consequence's possible upsides) and undesired attributes (the consequence's possible downsides).

When considering a decision, ask yourself, "If I make this decision, what are the (reasonably) possible consequences?" For each consequence, then ask in follow-up: "What is its potential upside? What is its potential downside"?

TO IMPROVE NOW

Thinking it a great idea, you are about to invite your significant other to join you in a fine dining experience at a nearby French bistro. However, based upon your readings in this book, you remember that consequences count, and that there is (almost) always time to think. Identify three reasonably possible consequences of issuing this invitation right now and describe at least one potential upside and one potential downside of each consequence. If this analysis takes you longer than a minute, you likely need more practice identifying reasonably possible consequences and their associated upsides and downsides.

Possible consequence	Upside	Downside
1.		
2.		
3.		

Two heads are (usually) better than one. People making decisions by themselves often have a narrowness of vision similar to that of a sentinel looking through an arrow slit in the wall of a Game of Thrones castle: "If I don't see a dragon out my window, I am tempted to conclude that dragons are not a threat anywhere." Discussing potential decisions with people who agree with you will contribute little to the quality of the eventual decision, much like asking a second guard at the castle, "Please look out my arrow slit and tell me if dragons are a threat."

However, I have found great value in discussing a possible decision with people whose opinions differ from mine—with people (figuratively) looking through an arrow slit on a different castle wall. I know that our differences in opinion usually result from one of two things:

- Our assigning markedly different values to the same consequences (e.g., it turns out that men assign widely differing values to different potential complications of prostate surgery; my values are not universally held). In this case, the next step should be a review of the considered values.

- One of us is considering a consequence that the other did not consider (i.e., the cost of prostate surgery will likely wipe out one person's savings, while having little effect on the person with excellent medical insurance). Here, the next step is a re-evaluation that includes full consideration of the missing consequence.

As discussed in "*Happy Birthday; Part Three (The Punishment*" (page 145), such conflicting opinions may be present even if you have not openly sought them out. Instead, they may simply raise a concern that you will need to "sell" your proposed decision to a hostile audience.

During my time at the West Point hospital, I learned that advisors were of more value to my decision-making when they carefully critiqued decisions I was considering than when they suggested new decisions. Since then, in a variety of settings, I have focused the efforts of a wide variety of patient advisory groups, client panels, and user representatives primarily on providing such critique. While I also make a point of listening to their ideas for "new stuff," I regularly emphasize that I need their input to minimize the chances I will make a stupid decision based upon some personal, too-narrow view of the issues at hand.

Note that this is slightly different from the issues involving experts when you are reaching a decision. Ideally, experts should use their "expected knowledge envelopes" to identify for you additional alternative decisions, unidentified possible consequences, or specific facts bearing on a decision. Thus, experts fill in your gaps with their unique knowledge. It is incumbent upon you to depreciate the value of the expert's advice when you believe it has been tailored to advance a parochial bias, or when it has been presented as "the only possible choice you have!" At the same time, do not abdicate your responsibility to decide simply because they are the expert, and that's what they said should be done.

TO IMPROVE NOW

Think of three examples of decisions you faced where you felt intimidated or manipulated into accepting a recommendation primarily because it was made by an expert. Looking back on each, how might you have reframed the question you initially asked of the expert so as to more effectively focus their response on some specific aspect of their expertise?

Decision faced	Expert advice given	Reframed question

TO IMPROVE LATER

At the next three opportunities, designate one or two of those involved in assisting you to consider a decision as the "Red Team." Charge them to develop the strongest possible argument *against* the decision you favor. Afterwards, did their work assist you in identifying the best decision? If so, what actions can you take to encourage others to intellectually challenge your thoughts as you reach future decisions?

Consider using an abbreviated decision analysis methodology. When I identify that a particular decision deserves more attention than it first seemed, my choice of strategies is one I learned at the Army War College. It requires creating a document that:

- Clearly states the problem
- Lists the possible decisions to be considered
- Identifies, for each listed decision, the most likely consequences
- Lists the potential upsides and downsides for each possible consequence
- Recommends one of the possible decisions, and defends that recommendation
- Solicits and adequately addresses critique by all involved parties

When the decision maker receives the completed document, it clearly presents any remaining disagreements between those who contributed to it. This strategy combines elements of the "weighing of possible consequences" found in formal decision analysis with the ability of multiple reviewers to detect errors of omission, commission, or interpretation made by the document's initial drafters.

I have found this process easily adaptable to decision-making by individuals in a wide variety of non-military settings, and especially in settings where coordinated action of multiple stakeholders is important to success. Most notably, I used this process as a founder of a venture funded start-up to plan for, to implement, and to the monitor the function of a quality assurance program involving more than 500 nurses working from five widely separated telephone call centers and providing real-time advice to callers with new or worsened symptoms.

Case Study 15 *"Just Say No"* (page 157) provides an excellent example of how such an abbreviated analysis can be presented.

TO IMPROVE LATER

Identify a recent decision you faced that had multiple possible resolutions. On paper, outline an analysis of the problem in support of what you believe to be the best resolution and identify its possible solutions; use the abbreviated version of decision analysis described above.

Chapter Summary

Conducting high quality decision-making in common personal and business settings does not require an MBA. This chapter has provided a primer describing techniques you can quickly learn to use efficiently and effectively. To assist you in remaining alert to your pre-stupidity alarm, the process starts with a nested series of questions that help you determine whether a decision deserves more consideration than initially allocated to it (page 61). Decisions that warrant further consideration can be guided by the five concepts discussed in this primer:

- There's almost always time to think
- You can avoid paralysis-by-analysis
- Consequences count
- Two heads are (usually) better than one
- An abbreviated version of classic decision analysis can be useful

Now that you have studied the tools, tactics, and techniques important in taming your Stupid Monster, you are prepared to employ those tools going forward in analyzing your own issues and situations. Because it is always useful to practice new skills in situations of relatively low risk (think: bicycle training wheels; boxing with a sparring partner; cooking that first soufflé for family, rather than friends), Part Three presents fifteen case studies that will further your efforts. By studying the actions of others as they faced—successfully and unsuccessfully—the opening snaps of their own Stupid Monster, you can try out what you have learned in a no-fault environment.

PART THREE

CASE STUDIES

INTRODUCTION

Each of the fifteen case studies that follow provide specific examples of issues important to understanding your personal Stupid Monster, the skills necessary to tame it, and strategies to facilitate better decisions. While all occurred in the setting of my five years as Commander of the Army hospital at West Point, I include each in this book because of its applicability to any setting. Each case study follows a similar format:

- Brief recitation of the story itself
- Discussion of the specific points raised by the story, referencing material discussed in detail in earlier chapters, and
- Sets of "To Improve" exercises to allow practice of new skills

For readers who just have to know how the story came out, each case study concludes with a short description of the story's denouement.

The exercises allow you to practice Stupid Monster taming in a relatively no-fault environment. The "Improve Now" exercises will be most effective if done before reading further, while the "Improve Later" exercises are designed to be completed at a time of your choosing.

I present these case studies in two groups. The first group presents situations in which the ability of the protagonist to detect the barking of their guard dog was potentially impaired by one or more of the traits, behaviors, and situations described in Chapter Four. The second group presents situations in which those involved utilized various decision strategies described in Chapter Five to reduce the likelihood of butt-bite.

As discussed at the end of Chapter Three, being able to recognize the warning bark of your personal guard dog is *the* fundamental skill; absent that basic ability, the real-life examples presented in these case studies, which are intended to amplify and enrich the issues developed in Chapters Four and Five, will likely be of little benefit to you. If you are not yet comfortable that you are aware of your tells, or however you sense that you may be making a stupid decision, go back right now to review Chapter Three and re-do the exercises.

CASE STUDY #1:

THE LAWN WORKER
Impaired by Behavior: Impulsiveness

This case study occurred years before internet-based social media platforms exponentially expanded the scope of "stupid" that can follow trying to be funny without thinking it through. As you will see, I made an impulsive response, and as a result I never noticed the opening snap of my Stupid Monster's jaws.

As discussed in Chapter Four (page 33), those plagued with impulsive behavior regularly act before even considering whether or not their guard dog might be barking. They routinely select the first decision that occurs to them, and so frequently make stupid decisions.

The old admonition "think before you speak" encapsulates the best defense against impulsiveness; however, today the "post" or "send" button on your social media app is as likely to cause impulsiveness trouble as is your mouth.

THE STORY

That Sunday, I was wearing work clothes and boots while digging out dandelions from the front lawn of our Army quarters at West Point. A top-down convertible stopped at the curb and someone from the passenger seat called out, "Oh, soldier. Does the Army make you do yard work for the officers?" Recognizing that as the opening line of an old Army joke, I reflexively responded with that joke's final sentence: "No, but if I do a good job the Colonel's wife lets me sleep with her."

The car pulled away, and I continued digging out dandelions.

I had forgotten the encounter by the time of the totally unexpected telephone call I received from the Deputy Superintendent's secretary "asking" that I come to his office "right away." His expression as I entered his office foretold that this was to be a less than pleasant visit.

As I stood in front of his desk, he held up what I could see was a two-page typed letter. He asked, "Barry, did you really tell some tourist family two Sundays ago that you were an enlisted man doing some colonel's yard work in exchange for sleeping with his wife? What in hell were you thinking? Here. Read this complaint they sent to the Superintendent!"

Reading the letter, I finally recalled the episode and realized the writer and I had interpreted it very differently. I had tried to be funny; he had heard an "off-color comment of the sort that has no place on the grounds of a national treasure like West Point."

To the Deputy Superintendent's opening question, I replied, "Thinking wasn't involved; it's an old joke, and the punch line just popped out my mouth without my thinking. He's taken what I said literally. I was joking, but obviously the letter writer saw no hint of that."

"Well, it was damn stupid of you, I'll grant you that," he responded. "What you're going to do now is to write this gentleman a very nice letter of apology. You'll bring it to me and I'll attach a personal note saying I have counseled you appropriately. Hopefully that will close it out amicably on all sides. But, Barry. You're in too senior a position here, and will be in your future assignments, to have the luxury of saying the first smart comeback that comes into your mind."

DISCUSSION

The whole experience brought to mind Dr. Sanford's comment regarding the genesis of stupid actions of young medical teachers: "The most common mistake of new junior faculty is to just say out loud whatever comes into their minds at the time, without any consideration of the possible consequences. It's as if their frontal lobes had suddenly atrophied" (page 10). In hindsight, I had acted in just that manner—an action followed by a clearly to-be-expected butt-bite.

TO IMPROVE NOW

Consider material you received or read over the past few days via e-mail, Twitter, Facebook, or other media platforms.

- Are there examples of messages that might have been intended as witty or funny by their author, but that you found off-putting in some way?
- Do you routinely ask yourself "how might this be misunderstood?" before sending an email or posting a message or comment? To avoid butt-bites, this is a good practice to instill.

TO IMPROVE LATER

The grid below presents a comparison of the benefits and potential downsides of the myriad of ways we now use our phones, email, and various social media platforms. Review the grid and note how many of the butt-bites you have personally experienced, whether on the sending or receiving end.

Benefit	Potential Butt-Bite
Receiving photos from families and friends	Accidentally sending a "just for you" sext to "all"
Resending interesting materials	Forwarding of your material by others to people to whom you do not want it to go
Sending the same message to multiple people with	Using the wrong addressee list to send the same

one key stroke	message to multiple people who you did not want to receive it
Texting sporting results in real-time "from the stadium"	Accidentally sending them to your boss who thinks you're home sick
Responding quickly	Lacking ability to "un-send" a response written intemperately
Forwarding a humorous message	Learning that one person's "humor message" is another's racial, religious, gender, or ethnic slur
Joining discussions with "like-minded" individuals	Being duped by "online companions"
Easily keeping records of all communications	Having old communications revisited or reviewed absent of their proper context

Then, consider whether your use of social media may involve impetuous behavior you would prefer to avoid. If so, list three specific things you can try over the following week to lessen your risk of social media-induced butt-bite. (See the example in Chapter Four of a "delayed send" function to prevent impulsive email responses.)

Considerations to Reduce Social Media-Induced Butt-Bite

1 _____

2 _____

3 _____

FOR THE CURIOUS: The Rest of the Story

We never heard again from the tourist whom I had so offended. I added "feeling like making a smartass comeback" to my personal list of tells that my Stupid Monster's jaws had snapped open.

PUSHBALL PUSHES BACK

Impaired by Trait: Lack of Moral Courage

The junior officers involved in this case study could have objected when their superior officer announced a decision with predictably undesirable consequences. Despite positional and professional obligations to speak up, each decided not to object, thus providing tacit assent to their boss's poor decision. By failing to "speak truth to power," they did not demonstrate the moral courage expected of them.

As discussed in Chapter Four (page 36), an insufficiency of moral courage impairs responding to the warning barks that should accompany consideration of a decision to not say something when saying something is expected.

THE STORY

In the summer following completion of their first (plebe) year, West Point cadets move from their barracks on the main post to the more rustic accommodations at Camp Buchner, a separate portion of the Military Academy about seven miles away. There, organized into platoons comprising four 11-member squads, they undergo what the Army calls "training in individual and small unit tactics." In addition to the strictly military training, there is a full schedule of organized sports events.

This summer training exercise is a hugely complex effort with a great number of moving parts. It involves effectively coordinating the efforts of many hundred cadre and support staff. The military is very good at producing the highly detailed training plans required to effectively carry out something like this. The thick "Buchner Training Plan" was revised each year, with its final form agreed to yearly by the leaders of all involved, well before training started. The Operations Plan for the Camp Buchner Summer Cadet Training clearly stated: "Except for emergencies, no changes to this plan are to be implemented without prior approval in writing of the Chief of Staff (COS), US Corps of Cadets."

As had been the case for more than a decade, the plan set aside time each afternoon of the first week for the staff to supervise eleven-person pushball intramurals. Intramural pushball at West Point was typically played on a football-like field by teams of eleven members each, without pads or helmet. The team goal was to move a five-foot diameter ball towards the opposing team's goal. The game starts with the ball placed at midfield in possession of one team, as in the start of a soccer match. Teams score points by moving the ball over the opponent's goal line, with additional points earned for pushing it between the goal posts below the crossbar, and even more points earned for heaving the ball over the crossbar between those uprights.

This summer, the Army major in charge of the intramurals program suddenly announced a plan modification to his staff. "I've decided to make a small change to the first week's intramural program. We'll still be playing pushball, but we'll make it into a tournament. Instead of the usual eleven on a side, we'll play platoon against platoon in a double elimination tournament fashion, until we have identified an overall champion platoon. Also, rather than using a coin flip to decide which team starts with the ball, we'll make it more physical by putting the ball in the middle of the field with each team lined up along its own goal line. At the starting whistle, they can race each other to gain control of the ball."

The junior officers on his staff accepted the major's changes to the approved training plan without comment.

The first pushball game of the afternoon resulted in one cadet hospitalized with a severe concussion, another in a cast for a broken upper arm, and eight other cadets with less severe injuries. Meanwhile, the major and his staff continued the pushball tournament. The second game sent a cadet to the hospital for surgery to repair torn knee ligaments, and another four cadets to the clinic with lesser injuries.

At this point, the military physician assistant at Camp Buckner called both the hospital leadership and the Camp Buchner commander to inform them, as required by the approved training plan, of an unusual pattern of injuries. He gave as his medical opinion that the injuries directly resulted from "unilaterally-approved changes to the pushball rules."

The Camp Buchner commander arrived at the pushball tournament in the middle of the third game and immediately stopped play. By that evening he had formally relieved the major of his role in the summer training program, an action that effectively ended the major's hopes for a successful future in the Army. He also counseled the junior officers that they had failed in what he described as their "obligation as Army officers to always speak truth to power."

DISCUSSION

The major at the center of this case repeatedly demonstrated both the depth and the persistence of his arrogance-based stupidity: 1) his decision to unilaterally change, absent an emergency, an approved training plan endangered all participants and led directly to the needless injury of multiple cadets; and 2) his refusal to modify his decisions after the first round of injuries caused his superiors to effectively terminate his career as an Army officer.

Each junior officer clearly had an opportunity to speak up when the major announced he intended to unilaterally make changes to the approved training plan, but each decided to remain quiet. As each considered whether or not to speak up, their Stupid Monsters' jaws snapped open for two reasons: 1) absent approval of the COS, the proposed changes violated the rules, and 2) the proposed changes needlessly endangered cadets. Unfortunately for the cadets (and probably for the major as well), a lack of moral courage prevented each of these junior officers from responding to their warning by speaking out. How different things might have been if, instead of saying nothing, one had said:

- "Major. If we're going to propose those pushball changes, we need to get them to the Chief of Staff, in writing, right away. According to the cover documentation, any changes to the Buchner Operations Plan require his approval in writing, and in advance."

- "Major. Under this format, there might be a few more injuries than usual. Do you want me to let the medical folks know we're making these changes in case they want to beef up their staffing?"

- "Major, I was under the impression that the point of the Buchner intramural program is to reinforce in the cadets' minds that this summer training isn't a competition between cadet units. Might not these changes undermine that?"

Had one of them voiced a concern following the major's announcement, it is quite likely that one or more of the others would have spoken up as well. In that case, the major may very well have retracted his decision, modified it, or offered it as a recommendation for review by more senior officers. Had any of those three things happened, the pushball competition would almost certainly have proceeded as in years past, with few cadet injuries, and a major's career would not have been terminated.

Taming your Stupid Monster includes recognizing and dealing effectively with situations where, by simply not doing anything, you are, instead, actually *deciding* not to do anything.

TO IMPROVE NOW

Recall the last three times someone made a decision that raised serious concerns or reservations for you. How easy did you find it to speak truth to power?

	Decision Raising Concerns	Easy	Difficult	Impossible
1				
2				
3				

TO IMPROVE LATER

For each of the above three situations, develop and practice out loud a statement that expresses to the decision-maker the basis for your concern (why your guard dog barked), but expresses it in a manner that does not directly attack the decision or the person who announced it.

FOR THE CURIOUS ... The rest of the story

I don't know what happened to the junior officers involved; however, I personally try to think of the needlessly injured West Point cadets whenever I find myself trying to decide whether or not to speak up when an announced decision triggers my guard dog's bark.

TOBOGGAN, OR NOT TO BOGGAN

Impaired by Trait: (Reverse) Bravado

Captain Early, worried that people would laugh at him for how he got injured, debated with himself whether or not to seek medical care for what an injury that he, as a physician, knew could produce serious complications.

Fear of exposure ("reverse bravado," as discussed on page 43) can powerfully impair the ability to hear your dog's warning bark.

THE STORY

In an earlier life, Captain Early was a Navy SEAL; now, after three years of residency following four years of medical school, he was the newest of four family medicine physicians assigned at the West Point Army hospital.

Not a skier, on a whim three weeks earlier he had purchased a used six-foot maple toboggan at a swap meet while buying skis for his son. Ten days before the incident, Captain Early had driven his young son to ski lessons on the small (a single tow rope and a single poma-lift) West Point ski slope located on a 750-foot rise just up the road from the hospital. Looking up at the graceful runs after the first heavy snow of the season, he had decided on the spot "that it would make a really great toboggan run!"

Now, on a beautifully clear Sunday morning (the first staff and patrons would not arrive for at least another hour), he had finished his toboggan-pulling climb to the top of the slope. Perfect time and place, he thought, for a toboggan ride!

After about 200 yards down the slope he realized he was in way over his head: moguls on the course repeatedly launched him and his toboggan into the air, and pine trees at the edges of the run whizzed by in a blur.

He was contemplating bailing out when he realized that he and the toboggan were no longer connected. He hit hard; landing on the left side of his chest, he both heard and felt cracking in his rib cage. After a thirty-minute descent on foot, while tightly holding his chest with his left arm to help splint what clearly seemed a couple of broken ribs, he reached the bottom of the run.

He then faced another decision: What to do now? Going to the hospital for evaluation would involve explaining how he had gotten injured, and, he realized, his story would not make him look all that bright, and would probably would be all over the command by the end of the day. "Maybe," he thought, "I should just go home and treat myself. After all, there really isn't any treatment for broken ribs except for wrapping the chest tightly to splint it and giving over-the-counter pain meds."

DISCUSSION

Having already made one stupid decision, whose consequences included broken ribs, Captain Early was now considering another. As a physician, he knew that the complications of broken ribs include life-threatening bleeding from a ruptured spleen and breathing difficulties from a puncture of the lungs. He would advise any of his patients with such an injury to be medically evaluated as soon as possible. However, here he was now, actually considering treating himself at home to avoid potential embarrassment.

Captain Early's desire to hide his earlier stupid decision from his peers and colleagues was impairing his decision-making, his concerns being essentially the reverse of the bravado behavior. The jaws of his Stupid Monster had now snapped open in contemplation of a second bite that day.

Whenever bravado (or reverse bravado) is entwined with consideration of a decision, the risk of butt-bite rises. That elevated risk should prompt recognition that the decision will require more thought than was originally allocated to it. Dr. Early's situation as he considered what to do next is among the reasons I have included the question "Is it likely that my ego or desire for self-protection is distorting this decision-making?" in the list of screening questions on page 106, along with three follow-up questions for consideration when this screening question is answered "yes."

TO IMPROVE NOW

Identify three situations in the recent past when, with the benefit of hindsight, you realize that a desire to avoid embarrassment (reverse bravado) significantly impaired your decision-making. Would asking and answering the screening question quoted above have allowed you to hear a warning bark indicating that the decision warranted additional time? If so, what actions can you take to make it more likely that you will ask that question as you consider future decisions?

TO IMPROVE LATER

Going forward, keep track of situations in which avoiding embarrassment is an element of your decision-making. If you identify five such situations occurring in less than a week, you have probably identified a reliable impairment to your being alerted by your pre-stupidity alarm. It will be worth your time to consider and develop strategies to ameliorate this issue.

FOR THE CURIOUS: The Rest of the Story

Captain Early decided to seek care at the Emergency Department. He had two broken ribs, but his spleen and his lung were fine. He recovered, despite the occasional ribbing by colleagues along the lines of, "They must not have covered tobogganing in SEAL school."

CASE STUDY #4:

DIAMONDS ARE FOREVER

Impaired by Behavior: High Emotion

In this case study, Lieutenant Lafferty, a nurse at the West Point hospital, having just gotten engaged, was beyond thrilled and wanted everyone to know it. She failed to realize that her exuberant happiness impaired her ability to hear the opening click of her Stupid Monster's jaws and, as a result, she was more likely to do something stupid.

Chapter Four discusses how being in the grip of strong emotion (page 40) can impair your ability to recognize the warning bark of your guard dog as you approach making a decision, thus depriving you of the opportunity to reconsider before acting stupidly. When you are emotionally wrought, it is hard to either wait for the emotion to subside or to trigger defensive hyper-vigilance, as Lieutenant Lafferty's experience will demonstrate. However, there are measures you can take now to reduce any future emotion-driven unawareness of your Stupid Monster's opening jaws.

THE STORY

West Point had a very clear rule prohibiting cadets from dating non-cadet service members stationed at the military academy. A cadet violating this rule would be kicked out, and the other service member would be quickly re-assigned to another base. The rule and the punishments were well known, but that did not discourage all such relationships. "Under the radar" and "stealthy" described those that did exist. As a senior officer at West Point, I was expected to report any violations of this rule of which I became officially aware.

This Sunday afternoon, Lieutenant Lafferty had accepted the proposal of—and a very large emerald-cut engagement ring from—Cadet Leyland while they were jogging together on a trail on Academy grounds. His subsequent sprained ankle had brought them to the hospital Emergency Department (ED). Now treated and sporting cast and crutches, he was seated in the waiting area wearing his cadet physical training gear with his name tag on it. She was wearing civilian running clothes and standing next to him.

Not in uniform, and taking a shortcut to my upstairs office, I entered the ED waiting area and noticed Lieutenant Lafferty bubblingly showing off an engagement ring to the ED staff. When she saw me, she turned, immediately extended her newly-ringed hand to me, gestured possessively towards Cadet Leyland who struggled to stand up, and said, "Colonel Wolcott. The best thing has just happened! Let me introduce you to …"

Had her warning system not been impaired by emotion, she would never have started to tell a senior officer of her engagement to a cadet. She would have known that to be stupid. Instead, oblivious to the warning snap, she was about to finish a sentence that would trigger a butt-bite and set into motion its consequences: his expulsion and her reassignment.

DISCUSSION

As I later considered the period leading up to Lieutenant Lafferty's about-to-be stupid statement to me in the ED, I identified three possible ways a properly warned Lieutenant Lafferty could have avoided a butt-bite.

- When she first received the ring, Lieutenant Lafferty could have said, "The ring is really gorgeous, but I think I should only wear it when it's just the two of us. I don't want to have to lie about who gave it to me, and I certainly don't want to see you expelled in your last few months before graduation."

- Lieutenant Lafferty could have said, "I don't think I should go with you into the ED, especially now that we're engaged. People are apt to gossip and get us into trouble."
- Lieutenant Lafferty could have said nothing to me at all; there was no reason she had to do so.

In a similar fashion, I identified how others might have helped an impaired Lieutenant Lafferty avoid a butt-bite:

- Cadet Leyland could have suggested she limit wearing of the ring to private times.
- Cadet Leyland could have suggested he go alone to the ED.
- Any ED staff member could have warned her that flashing her ring around was apt to get them both found out and into deep trouble.

TO IMPROVE NOW

Go separately to a family member, a friend, and a colleague and say something along the following lines: "I've figured out that I will probably make better decisions if I can avoid making them impulsively, or when I'm in a state of high emotion; I'd be glad if you'd call to my attention, if I don't seem to catch it myself, when I seem to be going off half-cocked." (It might be helpful to add a promise not to get upset when they raise the caution flag.) Put a note in your calendar to return to this issue in one month.

TO IMPROVE LATER

Did you receive any caution flags during the past month?

- If not, repeat and re-emphasize the importance to you of your requests.
- If so, did any of those flags cause you to modify your decision?
  - If not, did you at least avoid shooting the messenger?
  - If so, do you want to suggest similar caution flags to others with whom you interact?

FOR THE CURIOUS: The Rest of the Story

In the prior weeks I had heard gossip that one of the hospital nurses was seriously dating an about-to-graduate cadet, but as I had no official knowledge, I had taken no action and had begged to hear no more of the gossip. Thus forewarned, I was able to react just in time to Lieutenant Lafferty's words.

I held up my hand, cutting her off in mid-sentence, and turned to the cadet, saying, "I'm sorry, cadet. I was speaking to the lieutenant, here, not to you. No need to stand up, especially on a bum ankle. Please, sit back down."

To the duty sergeant I said, "Sergeant, please see that this cadet gets a ride back to the cadet area when you're finished with him."

To the lieutenant, I said, "Beautiful ring, Lieutenant. I'm sure there is a lucky guy somewhere who is every bit as happy as you seem to be; maybe I'll be able to meet him someday. Sorry you had to spend part of today in the ED." Then, in a louder voice, I said, "Hey, everyone, look at the lieutenant's engagement ring!" And I quickly left the area.

A week after that June's graduation, I received a formal announcement of the wedding of "First Lieutenant J. F. Lafferty (Nurse Corps), assigned to the West Point Hospital" to "Second Lieutenant L. P. Leyland (Infantry), recently graduated from the Military Academy at West Point." Handwritten on the announcement was a note: "Colonel Wolcott. Glad we didn't have to meet earlier. L.P. Leyland, 2LT, Infantry."

CASE STUDY #5:

HAPPY BIRTHDAY, PART 1 (THE CRIME)

Impaired by Behavior: Alcohol and Youth

In this case study, three soldiers set out to celebrate a 21st birthday, not comprehending how their combination of alcohol and the impetuosity of youth set them up for a dramatic encounter with the Stupid Monster, and a vivid lesson in the nature of consequences.

Chapter Four (page 33) describes how the incomplete brain development characteristic of younger individuals predisposes them both to act impulsively, and to inaccurately weight the possible consequences of their actions. Page 39 of the same chapter discuss how alcohol use does essentially the same thing, regardless of age. However, the combination of alcohol and youth produces a far greater effect than either alone; generally, the same amount of alcohol predisposes a younger individual to "do stupid" more often, and to a far greater degree, than it does to an older individual.

THE STORY

Three soldiers, planning a 21st birthday celebration for their oldest member, drove through light snow from their barracks to a liquor store, where they purchased three quart bottles of spiced rum—one for each of them. After taking a few celebratory nips before leaving the store's parking lot, they decided to drive to the on-base movie theater, see a Clint Eastwood movie, and continue the enjoyment of their spiced rum.

After many more nips in the theater, they started hurling insults at the actors, and at the several scores of cadets also attending the movie. Thrown out of the theater, the three found that in the time since they had parked, new snow and a brisk wind had combined to created snow drifts in the lot and on the nearby street. They decided to start the engine, warm up the car, finish their rum, and stay in the lot for the time being.

About 45 minutes later it was snowing a lot harder, the wind had gotten stronger, and each of the three had finished his bottle of rum. The appearance of 25-30 cadets exiting the theater and walking back to the nearby cadet barracks indicated the movie had ended. The soldier in the driver's seat put the car in gear, intending to drive back to their barracks about a mile away.

As he pulled out of the parking lot onto the street, the car skidded in the snow and swerved towards a knot of cadets. The cadets managed to get out of the way, but in doing so, several cadets fell into a snow drift. To the car occupants, that was hilarious! "Bet you can't do that again," one said to the driver.

As the driver sped up to take on the challenge, the soldier riding shotgun rolled down his window and began singing the Marine Hymn. Hitting the brakes when abreast of the next group of cadets, the driver reproduced the earlier skid and the cadets reproduced falls into the snow. Apparently finding all this "too funny for words," the three reprised their roles twice more as they left the cadet area and managed to leave behind two more groups of snow-covered cadets, several of whom had written down the car's make and tag number.

Alerted by calls from some very angry cadets, the Military Police eventually located the car, undamaged but stuck in the snow on a sidewalk near the enlisted barracks. In the back seat were three passed-out, vomit-covered young men who were soon identified as soldiers assigned to the West Point hospital. The MPs called the hospital's first sergeant and told him he could come to the station house to collect his soldiers "in a couple of hours when they have started to sober up." While the initial charge against each was simply "public drunkenness in offense to good order and discipline," the MPs said that other charges such as underage drinking, driving while intoxicated, and assault with a motor vehicle might be added later. These three soldiers were now potentially in very deep trouble.

DISCUSSION

I identified the following as points in this narrative where warning barks, had the soldiers heard and acted upon them appropriately, would have allowed for a far different outcome:

- Confusing celebrating with getting drunk: the former is acceptable in public, the latter is better done in private
- Choosing to drink in public places where alcohol was prohibited (the theater and the two parking lots), thus breaking the law
- Not identifying a designated driver before combining cars and alcohol, leading to the most serious of their legal problems: DUI and assault with a motor vehicle

TO IMPROVE NOW

If you have not already done so, place a ride-sharing app like Uber or Lyft on your smart phone.

TO IMPROVE LATER

Develop and practice out loud what you might say in a social setting where alcohol or drugs are in use to deal with being asked to:

- Decide on a location for a family reunion you don't want to attend, anyway
- Promote XYZ to the vacant position as Head of Sales
- Predict the upcoming fourth-quarter sales figures of your publicly traded company

FOR THE CURIOUS: The Rest of the Story

See Case Study 13, Happy Birthday, Part 3 (The Punishment) (page 145).

CASE STUDY #6:

HAPPY BIRTHDAY, PART 2 (THE TRIAL)

Avoiding Impairment by Setting: High Visibility

This case study describes the process I went through in deciding what type of disciplinary action to take against the three soldiers from the West Point hospital who, driving while drunk, chased cadets into roadside snowbanks (see Case Study 5, *Happy Birthday, Part 1 (The Crime)* (page 99)).

Chapter Four (page 33) describes how contemplating a decision in a high visibility setting can impair your ability to hear a warning bark. The arrest of these three soldiers placed me in just such a situation, and while aware of the intense interest in my decision, I needed to carefully think my way through to a butt-bite-free decision.

THE STORY

The three soldiers had been arrested by the MPs and, once they sobered up, released from jail. Now the issue was how to adjudicate the legal issues their behaviors raised.

This episode stirred up a great commotion at the Academy. Many cadets and Academy staff and faculty felt that this was a deliberate assault with intent to injure; several directly urged me to immediately recommend to the Academy Superintendent that the soldiers face felony charges at a court-martial, a recommendation falling within my options.

I also had the option to deal with these offenses as misdemeanors, employing a disciplinary hearing defined in the Uniformed Code of Military Justice as a Non-Judicial Hearing. At such hearings, a soldier's commander (in this case, me) serves as magistrate, hears evidence, renders a decision, and when appropriate, can impose combinations of loss of rank, limited fines, and short periods of extra duties as punishment. After a subsequent period of satisfactory service, commanders can choose to remove records of such discipline from a soldier's permanent record, thereby giving the soldier a fresh start.

DISCUSSION

I was leaning towards recommending court-martials but recognized that the high visibility of the case and the strong sentiment favoring severe punishments as a setting could impair my stupidity alert. I realized that the answer to the question "Is what I'm thinking of doing likely to get me butt-bit?" was "yes," regardless of the decision I reached. I went on to pose my six follow-on questions:

- Is it ethical?
- Is it legal?
- Is it likely that my/our ego is distorting this decision-making?
- Would it please my mother/boss/mentor?
- Would I be proud to read it on the front page of the paper, in my obituary, or on my tombstone?
- Is it non-selfish?

In this case, the answer to each was "yes," regardless of the decision. However, the answer to my third-level question, "Can I live with the worst thing that is likely to happen as a result of this decision," was "no" . . . if I recommended court-martial. At court-martial, the worst that could happen to the three soldiers was a felony conviction followed by hard jail time. That I couldn't live with. I concluded that the decision required more time; fortunately, there's almost always time to think, and this was no exception.

I felt I would benefit from the opinion of others, so I used some of the available thinking time to solicit the opinion of my senior advisor on enlisted issues: Command Sergeant Major James. He said, "Sir. These three fools get no credit for the fact that they didn't hurt or kill someone. That said, this was a drunken act, not a deliberate one, and was the act of three very young men during their first military assignment. Given all the free advice you're getting to send them for court-martial, it might be instructive to know what punishment the Academy would mete out to three senior class Cadets for a similar act."

I agreed.

Our review of cadet disciplinary records showed that alcohol-related incidents involving cadets were not uncommon. When such incidents occurred inside the grounds of the Academy, involved only other military individuals, did not result in injury to others, and were not complicated by obvious felonies, cases were almost always adjudicated without courts-martial; those found guilty could lose cadet rank, lose various privileges, and be assigned additional duty. Upon graduation and commissioning, records of such cadet disciplinary actions did not become part of their official military record. They started life as officers with a clean slate.

This cadet-centric system almost exactly mirrored the option available to me to deal with the three soldiers using a Non-Judicial Punishment Hearing. To me and to

CSM James, it seemed an appropriate decision to choose the latter. However, it also seemed certain to be viewed by many Academy cadets, faculty, and staff as a whitewash by the hospital commander.

Part 3 of this case study (page 145) examines and discusses the process by which I ultimately decided how to deal with this complex issue.

TO IMPROVE NOW

Can you identify a decision you had to reach while feeling as if in a spotlight aimed by opinionated onlookers awaiting their chance to become your open critics? If so, what was your response to that scrutiny? Did you rush your decision? Did you delay it? Did you vacillate based upon the currents of the group's opinions? Do you feel now that the quality of your decision was improved or diminished by your awareness of that environment?

TO IMPROVE LATER

Pretend you are drafting a press release to present and explain your decision. (Your minimum goal for this release is for even critics of your decision to accept the validity of your decision-making process.)

Complete the following: "When asked to explain the decision, he/she responded: _____."

Now, read what you just wrote as if you were among the initial "spotlight holders." How well would this paragraph deal with your concerns?

FOR THE CURIOUS: The Rest of the Story

See Case Study 13: *Happy Birthday, Part 3 (The Punishment)* (page 145).

CASE STUDY #7:

BEFORE YOU GO

Impaired by Setting:
Just One Last Thing

Everyone has been in the position this case study presents: receiving what could be a major ask—or even an order—cloaked as an innocent throw-away request at the close of an encounter. Unfortunately, when it happens, we rarely ask ourselves "What is the person trying to get me to do? What do they expect of me? How can I avoid the butt-bite this situation is likely to deliver?"

This case study describes my involvement in just such a setting, one I have historically found prone to dulling my responses to the warning bark of my guard dog. Like most of us, I want to please people. Being placed in situations like this concerns me; I worry that someone may be exploiting that otherwise admirable trait to manipulate my actions.

THE STORY

"Barry, before you go, just one last thing," said the Superintendent of the Military Academy as our introductory "get acquainted" meeting was coming to a close. "Our graduating seniors who have already been accepted to medical schools aren't getting awarded the Army scholarships they need as often as I think they should. They are among our best students academically, they get accepted to top ranked medical schools, and I feel they would all be great doctors for the Army. But especially in recent years, very few get selected for Army scholarships, and that means they can't go to medical school. I'd like that fixed. Would you take care of that, please."

In the two weeks since my arriving at West Point at the end of August, senior members of the hospital staff had been providing me with information on "topics likely to be of interest to the Superintendent when you first meet him." The information they provided focused primarily on specifics regarding the services the hospital I commanded provided to the West Point community, but also included in the briefings were materials related to other of my various responsibilities. Therefore, I entered the Superintendent's office already knowing the scholarship selections results. While I, too, felt them low, I had no explanation.

Because of my preparation by the hospital staff, I was able to respond, "Sir. The HPSP success rate for cadets over the past three years has hovered right around 45%. That seems low to me, as well. While I do not know why that has been the case, I'll examine the selection process in detail, report to you what I find, and propose any actions that the Academy could take aimed at improving that rate. I can't promise to fix it, but at the very least we'll learn the 'why'."

Rising from behind his desk and extending his hand, he said, "Barry, that sounds good. I know we can't change the results of the last round of HPSP selections; I just want us to do everything we can to better position next year's graduates. Find out what the problems are and give me your recommendations about resolving them. Thanks for coming in to see me."

DISCUSSION

At the Superintendent's use of the phrase "Before you go; just one last thing," my guard dog barked, as it should have! Experience has taught me that this, or one of its variants ("Now that I think of it," "That reminds me," and "While you are still here"), often introduces topics that are far from trivial to the speaker. In such cases, the speaker is manipulating the setting of the ask to make it more likely that you will respond with an unthought-through "Sure," "No problem," or "I'll be glad to." They intend the setting to dull your recognition of the warning bark, thus causing you to reflexively respond politely rather than deliberately.

I could not know what the Superintendent's goal was, but I recognized the setting as one that could impair my alertness to a barking guard dog. Therefore, I deliberately parried his ask by promising to look into his issue, being careful to select the most neutral language possible in so doing.

In this case, the Superintendent's reaction to my response quickly convinced me that he had not been meant his "please fix this" as an order to a subordinate to be quickly carried out. Rather, I saw it as a simple request to his "expert on medical stuff" to identify the problem's root cause and to suggest ameliorating actions he could take.

TO IMPROVE NOW

Identify three occasions when you have found yourself in a "just one more thing" situation. For each, recall whether you felt at the time whether the situation was benign or manipulative. Then, use the table below to also categorize each situation. Do these results mimic your impressions at the time the situation occurred?

Attributes	More Likely Benign	More Likely Manipulative
Power relationships between meeting participants	Participants are either power equals or the person bringing up the "one more thing" is less powerful	The person bringing up the "one more thing" is more powerful; the risk increases dramatically as the power difference increases
Nature of the meeting	Regularly occurring	Initial or abruptly scheduled meeting
Number of meeting participants	More than two	Only two
Nature of the "one more thing"	Clearly trivial and not controversial	Important and/or controversial
Your role in resolving the "one more thing"	Peripheral	Central

TO IMPROVE LATER

Once able (either innately or by using the above table) to accurately identify when the underlying nature of a "just one more thing" situation is likely manipulative, you need to have a practiced deflecting response ready to use. Draft such a response now; practice it out loud. (You may even benefit from reviewing it before entering a meeting where you judge the risk of encountering such a situation is high.)

FOR THE CURIOUS: The Rest of the Story

It took a while to figure out, but the root cause was that the official selection criteria for the HPSP scholarships rewarded applicants who worked more than twenty hours a week or played varsity sports as undergraduates, on the assumption that, given such a non-academic time commitment, their grades were even more impressive. Once the scholarship competition regulations were modified to similarly credit West Point cadets for the 30+ hours per week they were required to spend in military training and compulsory intramural sports, the cadets became equally competitive for the scholarships.

CASE STUDY #8:

DEER IN THE POOL

Impaired by Setting: Unicorn

In this case study, Captain Metkins, the officer responsible for training cadets in Military Survival Swimming in West Point's water training facility, is suddenly confronted with a unicorn situation (page 51). Failing to recognize it as such, and feeling the need as an Army officer to act decisively, he was unable to detect that his Stupid Monster was closing in for a butt-bite.

THE STORY

Major Hemming, the senior veterinarian at West Point and the hospital's Preventive Medicine Officer had been called to the swimming complex (which includes a full-sized Olympic swimming pool and 10-meter diving platform) by an excited sergeant working at the facility. The sergeant reported that a deer had entered the facility through a left-open exterior door, fallen into the pool, and was paddling around in the water. Major

Hemming arrived on the scene fifteen minutes later, just a few moments after the deer found a way out of the pool and staggered out of the building on its own.

Captain Metkins, the sergeant's immediate supervisor, arrived a couple of minutes after that.

After the sergeant described what had happened, Captain Metkins announced, "Well, that's just great! It'll have contaminated everything. We'll have to drain the whole damn pool and re-fill it. That'll take north of 600,000 gallons, take hours, and cost a bundle."

DISCUSSION

I'm pretty certain that had this been a question on a written test, Captain Metkins would have selected as his answer "Ask an expert for a medical estimate of the health risk" rather than "Immediately drain the pool." Why, then, when confronted with this unicorn situation, did he behave so differently?

Captain Metkins was unaware that being confronted by a one-in-a-million situation impaired his ability to detect his pre-stupidity warning bark, thus preventing him from recognizing his need to take more time than initially allocated to this decision. He had been well-indoctrinated during his time in the Army to view decisiveness as an essential characteristic of a good Army officer—indoctrination that generally fails to clearly distinguish decisiveness (effectively using the time available to evaluate possible decisions) from impetuosity or impulsivity (not using the available time effectively).

Captain Metkins was faced with a unicorn setting: deer simply do not go swimming in indoor pools! He had neither personal nor secondhand experience upon which he could expect to accurately estimate the magnitude of any health dangers the deer's brief swim might pose to future pool users. As discussed in Chapter Four, "unicorns" are among the settings that can transiently impair the ability to hear the warning bark.

- Given that there is almost always time to think, acting effectively in unicorn situations can generally allow resisting the temptation to respond reflexively or impulsively; instead, Captain Metkins succumbed to this temptation.
- What is clearly a unicorn situation for one person may for another be an event with which they have successfully dealt. In his decision-making, Captain Metkins failed to seek any advice from others.

TO IMPROVE NOW

Identify the personal tell (or tells) that arise when you face a unicorn situation. It may be as simple as hearing yourself say, "Damn! I have never seen anything like this before," or it may be as complex as your developing nausea or hives.

TO IMPROVE LATER

1.   Identify three unicorn events from your past, such as a strange social situation, a bizarre traffic accident, or even meeting a celebrity.

    • At the time, did you feel a strong urge to act decisively by choosing your response quickly?

    • Do you now think that you would have made a better decision had you taken a little more time to think things through?

    • Do you think you would have made a better decision had you asked someone with relevant experience for their advice?

    If you answered "no" to all three questions, it is unlikely that unicorn situations contribute significantly to any decision-making problems you face.

    However, if you answered "yes" to any of these questions, you will be a better decision-maker once you can reliably recognize when you have encountered a unicorn situation.

2.   Estimate your personal propensity for confusing impetuosity with decisiveness. If you are brave enough, ask three to five family members, peers, and subordinates to make the same estimate about you. If this exercise identified a problem, develop a simple strategy that will help you be less impetuous. (Personally, when I identified

this as a problem, I began telling people "I need to think, come back in three minutes," or were I by myself, turning over a three-minute egg timer sundial I kept on my desk for that purpose.

FOR THE CURIOUS: The Rest of the Story

Major Hemming introduced himself to Captain Metkins, pointed at the pool, and said, "The sergeant thought to call me when he was afraid the deer would drown. I don't see any deer scat floating in the pool, and even if it did urinate in the pool, that wouldn't be the first time a swimmer has done that. Besides, urine's sterile, and at best it would be a quart in several hundred thousand gallons of already chlorinated pool water. I really don't think, health-wise, you need to drain the pool. I don't see any medical problem. Just double-check in a couple of hours to be certain that the chlorine level stays in the correct range. I'll put that opinion in writing if that would help."

The pool remained undrained, the deer returned to the woods, and no one became ill as a result of the deer in the pool.

PIZZA PARTY

Failure to Consider the Consequences

The Emergency Department (ED) shift-leader sergeant in this case study did not recognize that the unusual situation presented by the sudden breakdown of a pizza delivery car had dulled her ability to note and respond to her guard dog's warning bark.

As discussed in Chapter Five (page 55), to avoid poor decision-making, you must consider possible consequences and weigh the upside and downside of each possibility.

THE STORY

As I arrived at the hospital for an unannounced late-night walk-through, I encountered a somewhat nervous ED shift-leader sergeant repeatedly glancing at the ambulance dock. Just then the ambulance backed up, the driver and assistant got out and opened the rear door of the ambulance, and rolled a gurney through the automatic doors from the dock into the ED. The gurney was stacked high with pizza boxes, food bags, and 2-liter soda bottles. The sergeant looked at me, shrugged, and said in her best "caught with a hand in the cookie jar" voice, "Sir. The pizza place's delivery car is busted. These guys had to return a cadet we had seen for a fever and cough to his barracks. Since it was only a little way farther, I told them to go ahead and pick up the food order at the restaurant after leaving the cadet off at his barracks."

I knew that it was standard procedure for the hospital's ED night shift to call in a consolidated group order to this local pizza place on behalf of everyone on duty in the hospital during that 11pm to 7am shift. The restaurant staff would deliver the order to the ED, whose sergeant would have taken the individual orders and collected the money. Those who placed an order could then pick it up from the ED front desk. The only difference this night was that the restaurant's delivery car was in the shop, and they couldn't deliver; only take-out was available that night. Because it was going so close to the restaurant anyway, the shift-leader sergeant had decided to use the ambulance and its crew, despite knowing such use was against regulations.

Clearly the sergeant's decision to use the ambulance had been followed by a Stupid Monster butt-bite: getting caught by her commander in full view of her subordinates. Equally clearly, she had not set out to make a poor decision. As she said, when we later discussed in private how things had evolved, "When I was making the decision I just assumed it would work out fine; I didn't stop to consider all the things that could go wrong, the potential consequences and their possible downsides."

DISCUSSION

The sergeant and I identified three possible consequences of using the ambulance to pick up pizza, and the potential upside and potential downside of each:

1. *No one notices, other than the ED staff.* The potential upside of this consequence would be that everyone gets their food order; however, the potential downside would be that the junior medics might learn the wrong lesson from the sergeant's action. They might internalize the lesson as: "It's OK to use government vehicles and personnel to run personal errands."

2. *Someone notices and complains about misuse of the ambulance and crew.* There is no potential upside here. The nature of the potential downside depends upon who complains, and to whom; the consequence could have been a newspaper headline saying something like: "Army ambulance and medics used to cater huge party while patients wait for care."

3. *Something bad happens to the ambulance and/or crew after leaving off the cadet, from accident to traffic stop*. Again, there is no potential upside. Any downside would occur in full public view, and the resulting newspaper headline could be along these lines: "Army ambulance on pizza run kills three in Highland Falls accident."

She recognized that each of this decision's possible consequences carried an unacceptable potential downside and said, "If I had taken the time to think it through like this, I'd not have done it." I agreed.

We also discussed the fact that as she made her decision to send the ambulance, she failed to ask, "Did I just hear the sound of my Stupid Monster's jaws snapping open? Is what I am thinking of doing likely to get me butt-bit?" Had she done so, she would likely have recognized that, knowing as she did that such a use of the ambulance violated regulations, the decision she was considering would be illegal; in that case she would have been well-advised to take more time than was initially allotted to consider it.

TO IMPROVE NOW

When was the last time you said about a decision of yours, "Had I considered the possibility *that* might happen, I'd likely have decided differently?" Why do you think you failed to identify that possible consequence of the potential decision and quickly weigh the potential upsides and downsides? Did you simply fail to see that consequence as possible, or did you (as did the sergeant in this case study) not go through a process to identify and weigh possible consequences?

TO IMPROVE LATER

Over the next week, make a written note in your journal of each time you deliberately considered the possible consequences of a potential decision to see if you could live with the worst one. Schedule time at the end of the week to conduct a formal review of the noted episodes and determine whether this methodology helped you make better decisions.

FOR THE CURIOUS: The Rest of the Story

The sergeant volunteered to prepare a 20-minute talk on decision-making in new-to-me situations, and to personally deliver it as part of the hospital's ongoing Non-Commissioned Officer's Professional Development Program. Unofficially, the story of what had happened (her being caught red-handed) and what happened (it was dealt with in private) rapidly became common knowledge.

CASE STUDY #10:

THE CASE OF THE PURLOINED INFANT SHIRTS

Decision Strategies: There's Almost Always Time to Think

At the time of this case study, Captain Gordon was in residence at the West Point hospital to complete the second year of a two-year Masters Program in Hospital Administration. He had yet to learn that, when it comes to making decisions, there's almost always time to think (page 57).

THE STORY

"Colonel. I've found a huge linen theft problem, and you need to act right now to fix it," Captain Gordon reported during the regular morning meeting of the senior staff of the West Point hospital.

"Gordie," said his boss and academic advisor, Colonel Kasper, "unless there's an armed robbery of our sheets and towels going on right now, perhaps you can let me and Colonel Wolcott in on the details after this meeting." Colonel Kasper's tone indicated pretty clearly to me that he felt blindsided by the captain's comments and was not happy about it. It also appeared that the captain was oblivious to the character of his boss's reaction. "Yes sir," replied the eager captain. "I have a full report already prepared."

A few minutes later, Colonel Kasper and I listened to Captain Gordon as he reported: "Sir. Over the past three years, this hospital's annual loss/replacement rate for the linen inventory item of shirts, newborn, has averaged 200%. The highest rate was two years ago at 245% and the lowest was three years ago at 187%. That's almost 20 times the loss rate of any other item in our linen inventory, and way above any loss/replacement rate that the Army Medical Department would consider acceptable."

(The "shirt, newborn" was a binder-like garment made of plain white cotton. Designed to cover a newborn from the diaper up, it tied on the side and exhibited failures of both form and function similar to its adult-sized cousin, the omnipresent hospital gown. According to Captain Gordon's data, the hospital was replacing its entire inventory of "shirts, newborn" more than twice a year.)

He wrapped up with, "Sir. I recommend that you act quickly by directing me to implement a program that will significantly beef up the control practices on this inventory item. Such a program will put in place tougher practices to bring the loss/replacement rate down to a tolerable level. You just can't allow this level of theft to continue."

"Is that your recommendation, too?" I asked Colonel Kasper. After a slight pause, he responded somewhat cautiously, "Well, since it's waited three years, it can most likely wait a bit longer. Rather than deciding something right this minute, why don't you let Captain Gordon and I pull together some more information, discuss it, and get back to you with a more specific proposal in another few days."

DISCUSSION

Colonel Kasper and I had (separately) learned through experience to generally view claims by others that some situation was an emergency requiring an immediate decision on our part as the opening snap of the jaws of our Stupid Monsters. We each worked from the belief that there's almost always time to think. His closing comments (above) to the captain were meant to validate the need for such thinking to take place before implementing any decision.

As discuss in Chapter Five many people already experience a muting of their pre-stupidity alarm resulting from their impaired ability to clearly distinguish decisiveness from impetuosity. A reduced ability to accurately identify when there is actually time to think permits impetuous decisions to be erroneously portrayed as decisive, on the illogical basis that emergencies demand decisive decision-making.

TO IMPROVE NOW/LATER
STILL TO BE WRITTEN

FOR THE CURIOUS: The Rest of the Story

When the two returned the following week, Captain Gordon made the following points:

- There were 250-300 babies born each year into military families cared for at the West Point hospital. The OB nurses said that parents routinely took their baby's infant shirt home with them as a souvenir.

- Review of linen management records revealed that the hospitals approved stockage level for shirts, infant was 150, and that losses required the purchase each year of 250-350 shirts at a cost of $1.69 each—a total cost that was a drop in the total bucket of the hospital's annual linen loss/replacement costs.

The captain added, "I see now that there was never a big theft problem; the problem was actually small in scope and not even classic theft. Colonel Kasper has taken the time to show me how to fully analyze a problem like this one; I'll need that ability in the future. But more importantly, he used this episode to show me that not everything labeled an emergency actually is; when someone says something's an emergency, taking time to consider my options is usually the first option I should consider."

Colonel Kasper had been an effective mentor once again.

CASE STUDY #11:

TOO MUCH OF A SURGEON

Decision Strategies: Don't Take a Rule for an Answer without Thinking

In a manner similar to all large organizations, the Army has rules, regulations, and policies intended to ensure that common processes overseen by many people and carried out in many locations are implemented uniformly. While promulgated with the best of intentions, slavish attention to such *diktats,* as discussed in Chapter Four (page 52), is an invitation to stupid.

In this case study, as Commander of the West Point hospital I dealt with a decision apparently mandated by such a regulation, when enforcing that regulation would require me to do something I felt stupid.

THE STORY

About three years earlier, the Army had decided that it didn't want "fat soldiers" in its ranks; a new regulation identified acceptable upper weight limits (by

131

height and gender) and mandated involuntary separation from the Army for soldiers who continued to exceed those limits after a specified period allocated for weight loss. One afternoon, paperwork arrived on my desk directing that I begin separating Major Shannon, one of two general surgeons at the West Point hospital, because he had failed to lose the necessary amount of weight to meet the regulation's requirements.

I knew Major Shannon to be an excellent general surgeon who was well-liked by patients and colleagues, and who regularly volunteered his time to supporting cadet intramural sports. Other than his inability to lose weight, he seemed to me to be an exemplary officer.

I also knew that the Army had subsidized his medical school education and had well-paid him as an active duty officer during his surgery residency. As a result of the Army's investment in his medical education and surgical training, Major Shannon was contractually obligated to serve eight years on active duty before he could resign; he still had seven years to go on that payback obligation.

Throwing Major Shannon out of the Army while he was still obligated to serve seemed stupid to me. If it separated Major Shannon now, the Army would lose his services for seven years, and the Army already had too few surgeons. Further, Major Shannon's debt to the Army would be canceled upon his separation, and he would be instantly employable in the civilian medical sector at two to three times his Army pay. In my mind, I heard the words of Br'er Rabbit: "Do anything else with me that you want, Mr. Bear, *but please don't throw me in that briar patch.*"

However, according to West Point's Military Personnel Officer, there was no other option. Calling to ask, I was told, "Sir, there just isn't any wiggle room in the regulation. He has to be involuntarily separated."

DISCUSSION

As explained in Chapter Four, settings where rules, regulations, or policies appear to require a specific decision frequently mute the ability of those involved to recognize a warning bark. In this case study, the Military Personnel Officer viewed the issue surrounding Captain Shannon as completely settled by the regulation's wording. In their mind, no alternative decision was possible.

When I am told, "You have to do XYX because the rule (or regulation or policy) says so," but my guard dog's bark warns me that doing XYZ is likely stupid, I make a deliberate effort to pause, take a deep breath, and consider that this decision probably deserves more consideration than first allocated to it. I start by asking, "Would the rule writer intend the rule to have this effect in this specific situation?" If not, I then ask three related questions to suggest a decision strategy I can use to deal with the issue:

- **Am I applying the wrong rule?** In such cases, the stupidity of applying that rule in that specific case would lie with me, not the rule writer. I can apply the correct rule and make an alternate decision without challenging the rule itself.

- **Have I failed to find an applicable exception within the rule's language that permits an alternative decision?** In such cases, the rule writer has already identified the possibility of the situation I am considering and has addressed it within the rule's fine print. The stupidity of failing to implement the rule's exception would rest with me, not the rule writer. Again, I can make a better decision without challenging the rule itself.

- **Did the rule writer not consider the specific situation I am facing, and so did not include it as a specific exception within the rule's language?** Because anything can happen, and eventually will, rule writers cannot think of or deal with every possibility that will ever occur. There will almost certainly be situations when exceptions to a rule must be entertained; the process by which they are entertained will vary with both rule and situation. In such situations, I have two options. I can request:
  o   A formal change to the regulation, or

o An exception to the policy for the specific case at hand

TO IMPROVE NOW

Estimate the portion of the decisions you routinely make that are influenced or constrained by existing rules, regulations or policies. If that portion is a third or less, feel free to skip the exercise immediately below. However, if that portion is greater than one-third, your decision-making will likely benefit from the following exercise

TO IMPROVE LATER

For the next week, keep a list of those decisions you make that involve or are constrained by a rule, regulation, or policy. For each of these, identify whether or not you worried that the decision recommended based upon the rule, regulation, or policy might actually be inappropriate for the specific situation. For each you felt might be inappropriate to the specific situation, did you conduct the three-question review recommended in the discussion above? For any in which you did not conduct that review, might your decision have been improved if you had?

If your analysis shows that conducting the three-question review would have improved your decision-making, create a plan to increase the likelihood that you will conduct such a review in the future. Try that plan for a month and return again to this exercise to evaluate your plan's effects.

FOR THE CURIOUS: The Rest of the Story

I decided to raise my concerns directly with the Office of the Surgeon General. I found it hard to believe they would want to involuntarily separate any Army physician who still owed service because the Army had subsidized their professional education and training. I put Major Shannon's involuntary separation paperwork in my drawer awaiting a reply to my inquiry.

It only took a couple of weeks to learn that commanders across the Army had voiced concerns similar to mine; across all elements of the Army, there were thousands of soldiers on obligated service to repay a variety of subsidized education and training opportunities of substantial value in a civilian setting. Of these soldiers, some were coincidentally overweight. Their commanders shared my dislike of throwing them into that high-paying briar patch.

Indeed, the people who originally drafted the regulation had simply not considered whether soldiers with remaining obligated service were to be involuntarily separated on the basis of their failure to meet the weight standards. Once aware of their oversight, they modified the regulation very quickly. Major Shannon remained on active duty.

CASE STUDY #12:

GENERATING SAFETY

Decision Strategies: Using Two (or More) Heads

Chapter Five describes using the question "Can I live with the worst thing that is likely to happen as a result of this decision?" as a safety net when considering a decision that has already set your guard dog to barking (page 61). This case study examines how a group can contribute in a good way to that consideration.

THE STORY

On the day I assumed command of the Army hospital at West Point, the Deputy Commander for Administration led me on a lengthy tour of its every nook and cranny. Opening a locked door in the basement, he revealed a mammoth piece of heavy machinery of no immediately obvious purpose. I was told it was "the hospital's diesel emergency generator.

It's here to take over if our outside power is ever knocked out, but I don't think that has ever happened."

Never had I considered that I would one day be responsible for knowing how to manage an industrial-sized emergency generator. I knew nothing about them. However, it was my first day in command and I did not want to openly reveal any sign of ignorance on any topic—especially in this case, where the staff must have had regular, first-hand experience with this piece of their hospital's equipment. Trying to project an understanding I knew I did not have, I proclaimed: "Those generators are really complicated pieces of equipment." Searching for something leader-like to add, I then said the first thing that came to my mind: "When is it next scheduled for testing?"

"I'm not certain, but I'll find out," was the Deputy's reply.

At a subsequent staff meeting, he told the group, "The post engineers agreed that they are responsible for maintaining our emergency generator; they'll be coming next Monday morning to test it. What they will do is cut the external power to the hospital, watch the emergency generator kick in, monitor the generator as it comes to full power, and confirm that it energizes the emergency power trunk lines to the care areas. Then they'll shut it down and reconnect the external power. Should take about 30 minutes."

The Chief Nurse quickly spoke up, his tone somewhat nervous, "Then I guess I'd better make sure that on Monday morning all the ICU monitors and ventilators are plugged into those circuits. We don't want the testing to actually kill any of the patients." (Throughout the hospital, specific electrical wall receptacles had yellow faceplates with the words "Emergency Power" imprinted along each plate's top and bottom edge, just so the medical staff could make certain that key equipment was connected to an uninterruptable power source and avoid the mistake he had voiced . . . and the catastrophic results of such a mistake.)

Then someone asked, very seriously, "What will happen in the operating rooms? Is everything there on emergency power?" Someone else quickly added in the same concerned tone, "How about the newborn nursery?"

Earlier, I had assumed I was the only one on the hospital senior staff who didn't know how all this emergency power stuff worked, and had tried to bluff my way through. Their comments made me question my earlier assumption. "How many of you," I queried, "have been here during a test of this system?"

Lots of looking about. No hands went up. We were individually and collectively emergency power neophytes.

"Well," I said to the group, "this testing may well not be as good an idea as, in my ignorance, I earlier assumed it to be. Multiple heads are often better than one; let's ask ourselves this key question: What are the worst things that could happen if we go ahead with this testing?"

In but minutes they had written a worrisomely long list on the conference room's whiteboard:

1. The system might not recognize the failure of the outside power source, and therefore not initiate the generator start sequence
2. The generator might not start
3. The diesel fuel may have become contaminated and foul the generator
4. The generator might not actually produce as much power as its design specified
5. The yellow wall plates might not correctly identify circuits actually connected to the generator
6. Staff might not be sensitive to which medical equipment needed to be plugged into the yellow receptacles
7. Critical parts of the hospital's lighting system, such as those needed at night, those in dark spaces like bathrooms and storage rooms, and those in basement rooms, might not work

This incomplete list of possible downsides to testing as planned demonstrated pretty clearly that the only possible upside to that testing would be if nothing really bad actually did happen to any patient. Not an acceptable risk/reward ratio.

We needed to think all this through a good deal more before we could be certain that we would not be putting our patients at risk. All agreed that testing of the hospital's emergency generator had to be delayed.

DISCUSSION

The initial comments at the staff meeting made my warning dog bark. Heeding that warning, it was clear to me that the decision regarding generator testing would require more consideration than I had originally allocated. Fortunately, there is almost always time to think. I elected to collect the group's thoughts of each item on the whiteboard, certain that each person might well identify one or more consequences not foreseen by the others.

There is a secondary, but important, message in this case study. My arrogance that first day in command—my new-commander's desire to appear "all-knowing"—and my encountering the unexpected issue of the diesel generator combined to blunt my ability to recognize the barking of my watch dog. In fact, no one at the hospital expected their new commander to be an expert on diesel generators. A far better response on my part that first day would have been something like: "Wow. I don't know the first thing about generators. Who on our staff does?" Identifying that the hospital lacked any in-house expertise would have better re-framed the problem from one of testing the generator to testing the whole emergency power system. Also, by openly acknowledging that I didn't know something, and then asking, "Who does?" I would have given tacit approval to others to be equally honest with me and among themselves in the future.

TO IMPROVE NOW

Identify three times when you have bluffed your way through a situation because you did not want to appear weak or uninformed to those in your company, but where you now realize your lack of knowledge did not represent a legitimate failing on your part. Create a response that does two things:

- Acknowledges that you do not know and that you do not feel diminished by not knowing, and
- Leaves the recipient with the feeling that you will be tolerant of (and in fact encourage) similar acknowledgments when made by others

TO IMPROVE LATER

Observe your family, friends, and colleagues as they consider a decision, looking for poker-like tells indicating that they may be receiving (even sub-consciously) warning of the approach of their Stupid Monster.

- When you identify one, deliberately engage the person in a discussion of the upsides and downsides of the decision under consideration
- Consider how you might use the sounding of *their* alarm to help *you* make better decisions

The next five times you face a decision-choice, list the upsides and downsides of each choice and then:

- Bring three associates together as a group
- Ask them to help you analyze the decision choices, and
- See whether their list of upsides and downsides improves on yours

FOR THE CURIOUS: The Rest of the Story

What started as a simple question became more complicated when we found that the only testing ever done was to demonstrate that the generator would come online when the outside power was interrupted. The process did not test whether the generated electricity powered the correct in-hospital circuits.

We engaged an Army-approved consultant, and together we created a multi-stage testing sequence that took place over about six months. During that time, we identified and corrected multiple previously unknown deficiencies. Had there ever been an actual external power failure (or, had we gone on with the proposed testing by the West Point post engineers), any one of these deficiencies could have seriously harmed patients:

- Many outlets identified as connected to emergency power actually were not; equipment plugged into them during a power failure would stop working
- The yellow faceplates identifying circuits as connected to emergency power were hard to locate in the semi-dark of a power failure
- Several areas of the hospital critical to patient care lacked functioning emergency lighting; and
- Staff training to deal effectively and safely when on emergency power did not exist

It was more than a year after I took command that we were able to add routine quarterly testing of the hospital's emergency power system to our ongoing efforts to make sure things actually worked.

CASE STUDY #13:

HAPPY BIRTHDAY, PART 3:
THE PUNISHMENT

*Decision Strategies: Considering
the Opinions of Others*

As I describe in this case study, I certainly did not lack for advice as to how to deal with the three soldiers whose drunken driving had put many cadets at risk that snowy evening. Most favored a court-martial, but after some thought I found that "I could not deal with the worst consequences of that decision, which would be hard jail time for the three.

Chapter Five discusses seeking and utilizing the recommendations/opinions of others as you make decisions. As you consider a decision, identifying the root cause for differing recommendations you may receive will improve your decision making. The root cause of conflicting recommendations is generally a disagreement regarding the value of the same consequence, or identification by one party of a consequence not considered by the other. Either merits your attention prior to implementing a decision.

THE STORY

Proceeding via a Non-Judicial Punishment (NJP) Hearing seemed to me an appropriate decision, but the strong countering recommendations for court-martial from members of the West Point staff and faculty and the Corps of Cadets served as a warning bark. However, I could not identify the root cause of their strong opposition to my proceeding with an NJP Hearing.

Since there is almost always time to think, I asked a close friend, an infantry officer with a stellar combat record who was now a full professor on the West Point faculty, "Why do so many people here want to see these three soldiers sent to a military prison?"

His response was, "They don't, really. The real issue for them is a fear that as a doctor, you might not be up to handling this correctly. You need to understand that, to most of them, you are more a doctor-in-uniform than a soldier in command. They are afraid your actions will be more therapy than punishment. If they were handling this in a unit they commanded, they would go the NJP route, too. They worry that you'll get it wrong, and just slap their wrists."

That was it! That was the element I had missed as I placed values on possible consequences in this complex puzzle.

DISCUSSION

I needed to successfully address concerns that, because I was a doctor in command, I would not be able to deal correctly with the NJP process and, as a result, these soldiers would escape appropriate punishment. In my evaluation I had never considered the factor my colleague raised.

My task was now clear: before conducting the NJP Hearing, I needed to convince these doubters that I would get it right. I needed to "sell" my decision.

CSM James volunteered to handle the convincing for me, off the books via the unofficial, but influential, network of senior non-commissioned officers at West Point. He showed each of them the information he had collected regarding the punishment of cadets found guilty of similar misconduct. More importantly, he affirmed his professional observation that "Colonel Wolcott runs a really tight NJP Hearing." He invited them to attend or to send a representative to the hearing to verify that description. In a parallel manner, I invited both the West Point faculty and the Corps of Cadets to send representatives to the open hearing.

At that hearing, the three soldiers admitted to the charges, apologized to the cadets attending the hearing, attested to lessons learned, and tearfully awaited their punishment. I asked the cadets attending the hearing if their peers, if ever in similar circumstances, would expect to be court-martialed and expelled from the

Academy. They agreed that cadets in similar circumstances would not. When I asked what punishment such cadets could expect, they said that a typical punishment would be loss of cadet rank, loss of most privileges, and hours of their limited free time instead spent walking the punishment area in full dress uniform with rifle.

In my final comments, I noted that the three young soldiers differed from Academy cadets primarily in their route into uniformed service and level of post-high school education. I stated that I intended their punishment be every bit as severe, but no more, as the punishment they would likely have received had they been cadets admitting to the same acts.

Therefore, having found the three soldiers guilty, I reduced each of the three in rank, fined them each a quarter of a month's pay for three consecutive months, and assigned them many hours of extra duty. I emphasized that they could get their record scrubbed by future good performance, but that I would be maximally intolerant of any future misconduct.

TO IMPROVE NOW

Identify three time recently when, while considering a decision, you have felt that a decision you made would require extra hard work in advance to sell it, spin it, or dress it up before announcing it to some constituency to avoid their opposition from the get-go.

In these three cases, should you have given more time to the decision than you did? If so, you have likely now identified a powerful personal tell. When you recognize this need to sell your decision, your tell should warn you to take more time, and to search for and deal with the root cause of the dissatisfaction you must sell to overcome. Now go back to page 31 and add this important tell to your list.

TO IMPROVE LATER

Mark your calendar to return to consideration of this issue in one month. At that time, identify any decisions that, once made, required you to subsequently work really hard to sell it to some of those affected. If you can identify more than a couple such decisions, you probably have not yet well-incorporated into your decision process an understanding that seeking out the root causes of negative comments of other heads is likely to improve your decisions, thus reducing the need for post-decision selling.

FOR THE CURIOUS: The Rest of the Story

The invited observers reported to their various constituencies that everything had been done strictly by the book; no longer was NJP Hearing versus court-martial a topic of conversation.

Through a combination of hearing the warning bark of my guard dog, detecting that this decision needed more time than had been initially allocated, determining the root cause of conflicting recommendations, and seeking input from a second head, my final decision seemed to have best balanced the needs of all involved.

CASE STUDY #14:

WISDOM TEETH WISDOM

Decision Strategies: Dealing with Expert Opinion

As discussed in Chapter Five, knowing how to assess an expert's opinion in a specific setting can be problematic (page 64). "After all," says the small voice in your head, "they are the expert. Who am I to overrule them?"

In this case study, the Chief of Surgery, his opinion sought as the hospital's senior staff expert on "things surgical," instead provided a recommendation based upon his personal biases.

THE STORY

Army regulations prohibited commissioning individuals with impacted wisdom teeth, because these teeth, still under the gum and stuck under a functioning rear molar, frequently became abscessed. Since impacted wisdom teeth are a common problem among college age individuals, an oral surgeon (a dentist with four additional years of training) was assigned to the West Point hospital to extract the impacted wisdom teeth of senior cadets, thus allowing them to be commissioned as lieutenants at graduation.

Colonel Poulis, the hospital's oral surgeon, had a very busy, if not terribly diverse, oral surgery practice. Each September, everyone in the West Point senior class had a medical examination which included dental x-rays. Each year, those x-rays identified about 250 cadets with impacted wisdom teeth requiring extraction.

He then began scheduling the cadets for surgical removal of their one to four impacted teeth; he could operate on about sixteen cadets per week, and usually finished about six weeks before graduation. He performed these extractions afternoons under local anesthesia in his clinic in the hospital, after each cadet's final class of the day. The cadets waited in the clinic afterwards to ensure any bleeding had stopped, and then returned to their barracks with advice for a full day of bed rest, ice packs, soft food, and codeine tablets. On the third day they returned to the clinic for a follow-up visit.

Colonel Poulis now requested that he be allowed to admit these cadets following their surgery, instead of returning them to their barracks. He supported his request by stating that, were the cadets admitted rather than sent back to their barracks, he could provide them with more powerful pain relief, ensure that they were able to ice their jaws (ice was hard to get in the barracks), give them IV steroids to reduce the swelling, and ensure that they had access to soft food. He believed that this regimen, in addition to being better post-operative care across the board, would reduce the number of academic classes these cadets missed in the days following their surgeries. To do this, he would need hospital admission privileges, a status allowing a provider to admit patients to a hospital and direct their care during that admission. At the time of his request, only physicians (MD or DO) were permitted to admit patients to the West Point hospital.

I had to decide whether or not to approve his request. If approved, it would significantly increase the number of daily admissions to this small hospital; that, in turn, would require changes in procedures across most of the hospital elements, from nursing to laundry. I sought the opinions of the hospital's senior medical, nursing, and administrative staff.

The nursing and administrative senior staff quickly found solutions to any concerns they identified, and recommended approval of Colonel Poulis' request. However, the Chief of Surgery, a physician, was vehement in his opposition—opposition he made official in a lengthy written submission to me. Although surrounded by a host of minor objections, his rationale, at its core, was simply that only physicians should have admission privileges to hospitals. Checking unofficially, I found no support for his position among other of the hospital's physicians with admitting privileges.

DISCUSSION

As discussed in Chapter Five, expert advice is often of great assistance in reaching good (or, in any case, "least bad") decisions.

Experts can:

- Identify alternative decisions not otherwise considered
- Provide technical information unknown to you that has bearing on the decision
- Identify otherwise undetected consequences of a potential decision

However, the proper role of an expert is to assist you in reaching a higher quality decision than you might otherwise reach, not to make the decision for you. An expert's opinion should be only one element you consider.

I find that considering such individuals as advisors, or as subject specialists, rather than as experts helps me keep their proper role clear. As I consider the advice of such subject specialists, I work to remember that their recommendations should:

- Not extend to areas outside their special knowledge area, unless specifically asked
- Not be thinly disguised directives

- Not misuse their position to present personal bias disguised as expertise

Experts' advice and analysis is usually based upon specific knowledge and experience they possess that you do not. That does not mean that their recommended decision is the only choice you have. They are neither witches nor warlocks; they are simply advisors to be used to improve your chances of avoiding butt-bite.

TO IMPROVE NOW

Identify three recent decisions you reached after receiving advice from an expert as you considered your options. Did you feel any extra pressure to follow that advice because it came from an expert?

- If so: How did you deal with that extra pressure as you made your decisions?
- If not: How would you have dealt with an expert had they applied pressure by saying something equivalent to, "I'm your lawyer, and I'm telling you that you don't have any choice but to do X."

TO IMPROVE LATER STILL TO BE WRITTEN

FOR THE CURIOUS: The Rest of the Story

I approved Colonel Poulis' proposal and granted him hospital admission privileges. Everything went as he had predicted. In fact, the rate of missed classes following wisdom teeth surgery fell by 90%, and at an awards ceremony six months later, the Academy leadership took formal note of Colonel Poulis' "significant contribution to both cadet health and cadet well-being."

I had a discussion with the Chief of Surgery explaining my view on the role of subject specialists, and how he could be of the greatest use to me in such a role in the future by separating his personal biases from his expert knowledge.

CASE STUDY #15:

JUST SAY "NO"

Decision Strategies:
Abbreviated Decision Analysis

Command Sergeant Major (CSM) Jonas, the senior sergeant on the staff of the West Point hospital wanted me to significantly alter the mandatory urinalysis drug screening program at the hospital.

Anticipating my resistance, CSM Jonas presented his analysis and recommendation using an abbreviated decision analysis methodology, as described in Chapter Five (page 67). This abbreviated method of analyzing and evaluating decision options is applicable to issues in any setting. Its essential steps are:

- Clearly state the problem
- List a finite number of possible decisions
- For each decision, discuss the advantages and disadvantages of their possible consequences
- Select (or recommend) one of the identified decisions and explain that action

THE STORY

The Army's mandate for unannounced urine drug testing to identify cannabis, opioid, amphetamine, and tranquilizer use was but a few years old at this time. The applicable regulation required every soldier to provide a urine sample at least yearly on an unannounced basis and under observation. Also mandated was a strict chain-of-custody documenting the sample's proper identification and submission to a central forensic-quality laboratory for testing. Commanders were to make use of the results of this testing for local disciplinary actions. At this time, local commanders retained considerable discretion as to those disciplinary actions for first-time offenses by very junior soldiers. Repeat positive testing, or positive testing by officers and sergeants, normally led to their forced separation from active duty.

Early in my tenure, CSM Jonas scheduled time to make a formal presentation to me as hospital commander. He started out by saying, "Sir. At the end of this presentation I will recommend that you change your Commander's Emphasis regarding the mandatory urinalysis program from one emphasizing detection to one emphasizing prevention. If you accept my recommendations, we will begin randomly testing everyone a minimum of three times a year. Also, speaking as Commander, you will describe the changes as an expression of your belief that mandatory testing is not intended to catch bad guys. Rather, it is to provide an easy excuse—this new testing frequency—for any staff member under pressure to casually use drugs, and allow them to do what they were already inclined to do: just say no.

As he started his presentation, he handed me a copy of his presentation, which included all elements of the abbreviated format:

1. Statement of the problem

What is the most effective manner in which this command can implement the Army regulation requiring universal urinalysis screening to achieve the regulation's goal of fostering a drug-free command environment?

2. Potential Decisions

1. Continue to emphasize that unannounced urine testing of our soldiers is intended to reduce use of cannabis, opioids, or amphetamines by detecting and punishing a small number of users.

2. Modify the structure of (and the stated rationale for) the testing program so that it best supports the current baseline intention of most individual soldiers to not use drugs.

3. Advantages of Potential Decision #1

- Current practice is totally in compliance with existing Army procedures; therefore, this command is essentially immune from outside criticism of how we do it
- Future results are easily predicted: we will likely continue to have to deal with three to five positive tests each year
- Requires no changes from current practice

4. Disadvantages Potential Decision #1

- Our urinalysis results over the past two years show that the current mandatory urine testing policy has not reduced what has always been a very low baseline rate of drug use in this command
- The current policy is a punishment-based method of behavior modification; such methods are generally ineffective in extinguishing unwanted behaviors that are uncommon
- Our current practices imply that, as hospital commander, you view the staff as generally predisposed to use drugs and believe they will be dissuaded only if sufficiently afraid of getting caught

5. Advantages of Potential Decision #2

- The reinforcement-based nature of this method of behavior modification is appropriate to encouraging behaviors that are already commonplace; it is the correct method for encouraging continued drug-avoidance in a group where abstinence is already common

- Individual soldiers, most of whom are already disinclined to use drugs, can use the existence of mandatory urine screening as an additional "excuse" to resist external drug-use pressures. They can say, "Well, I might want to try it, but my commander's urinalysis policy is so tight, I really don't dare. He's a real hard-butt on drug use."

- The few soldiers who are predisposed to use drugs will continue to be identified; the increased frequency of testing might actually make even some of these reconsider drug use

6. Disadvantages Potential Decision #2

- Increased time and expense of collecting and sending for testing 3-4 times as many urine samples as currently

- Individuals external to the command may criticize this as "changing something that already works well"

He closed with a re-statement of his recommendation and asked if I had any questions; I did not.

I told him I would need a few days to think about his analysis and recommendation, and that I would likely ask him to present his work to other members of the hospital's senior staff so that I could hear their thoughts and advice.

DISCUSSION

Rather than presenting a parochial recommendation for me to accept or to approve in isolation, CSM Jonas analyzed his recommendation using a structured decision format. In that format, the issues were clear, as were the individual elements that CSM Jonas had taken into consideration in reaching his recommendation. While I subsequently sought the opinion of others who might be affected by his proposed change, they could present their thoughts within the effective framework CSM Jonas' work provided.

I have found that this formal but abbreviated decision analysis methodology retains most of the advantages of its ultra-rigorous, mathematically based cousins while taking far less time. Also, I can follow it without getting lost in the math.

TO IMPROVE NOW

Identify a decision regarding a moderately complicated issue that you arrived at recently after listening to the recommendation of someone else, whether a family member, friend, or colleague. Was that recommendation presented in a manner that allowed you to easily analyze the underlying rationale of the person making the recommendation, or did you have to spend a great deal of your time trying to uncover whatever thought process was behind the recommendation?

Now, identify the last time you made a recommendation to someone regarding a moderately complex issue. Was your presentation sufficiently transparent that the listener could critique your analysis without themselves doing additional fact finding?

If your response is "yes" in either situation, you may well benefit from using this abbreviated version of classic decision analysis, and from endorsing its use to those making recommendations to you.

TO IMPROVE LATER

Put the following reminder into your calendar for a month from now: "In the past month, have I made any use of the abbreviated classical decision-making process, either in my presentations, or in those others made to me?" Follow up with these questions:

- If so, and if it helped, how will I ensure its continued use?
- If so, but if it didn't help, do I wish to abandon it? (If not, how might I modify it to perhaps be more useful?)
- If not, what can I do to give it a try over the next month?

FOR THE CURIOUS: The Rest of the Story

After hearing the comments (mostly positive) of other senior hospital staff, I implemented CSM Jonas' recommendations. I spent considerable time repeating that the increased testing was to "make it easier to say 'no,' not to catch more people." CSM Jonas and I were tested every time, decreasing complaints that the extra testing takes too much time from work. The already-low rate of positive tests even fell slightly. Interviews with hospital staff leaving for civilian life or new Army assignments revealed that many were proud that the hospital's testing program was so strong. A few said that the policy had been "important to my not using drugs while assigned here," and none complained that the policy had overly burdened them during their assignment at the West Point hospital.

PART FOUR

ADVANCED STUDIES

CHAPTER SIX
IT'S STILL ABOUT YOU; NOT THEM

As the manuscript for this book evolved, I was struck by how many readers of early drafts said, "Those attributes you describe in Chapter Four as potentially making it difficult for me to hear the warning bark of my personal guard dog? In fact, one (or more) of those perfectly describes my arrogant boss/distracted sibling/always-angry parent/impulsive teenager/always-policy-quoting friend/show-off office colleague. How do I get them to stop acting that way?"

My initial response to these comments was to say: "You don't get it. This book is about you learning to lessen the burden of your own stupid decisions; it's not about how to control others." Then, one of them put the issue this way:

"My boss is really a jerk! How do I get them to change?"

When I asked what it was about the boss that identified them as a jerk, I was told, "Almost every time I am called into in a one-on-one meeting in their office, they pull that 'Just one more thing before you go' crap you described; then they just dump some huge new task onto my plate with no warning and no discussion. Not only that, but they act as if they just thought of it, when I know the idea has been under consideration for some time. They assume it's really no big deal for me to fit whatever they ask into my to-do list, and act as if 'I couldn't possibly object' to doing a little thing like this for them."

When I pointed out that I had made specific recommendations for dealing with this issue in Chapter Three and in Case Study 7 they said, "Sure, if it just happened once in a while, I could deal with it that way, but it's almost every time. What infuriates me is to have my boss deliberately manipulate me like that over and over again. I get so mad that when it happens, I rarely remember to ask for sufficient details to actually do the task well. It's gotten to the point that when I'm called to their office, I get mad way before I even open the door because I just know they will be doing it again. I've even started brooding about it when I'm completely away from the office. I'm starting to hate going to work because of this. How do I make them stop being manipulative like that?"

As I considered my response, I realized that, while they identified the problem as their boss's recurrent manipulative behavior, they were actually experiencing difficulties dealing with their own stupid monster:

- Initially, they either failed to recognize that their growing anger to their boss's recurrent use of the phrase "Just one more thing before you go" was actually a warning bark of their guard dog (or they failed to react appropriately to the bark). Rather than seeking alternatives, they repeated undesirable decisions, such as not asking sufficient questions about each request, at each occurrence.

- Further, much like Pavlov's dogs who, hearing a bell rung prior to every feeding, eventually began to salivate upon simply hearing the bell, they began getting mad when simply called to see the boss, even absent the "just one more thing before you go" stimulus.

- With time, their anger globalized. No longer was the response restricted to simply being called to see the boss; now the response was diffusing uncontrollably to involve other work and even non-work settings. Unable to recognize and deal with this anger as a globalized warning bark and seek better alternatives, they resorted to labelling their boss as "a manipulative jerk," while accepting that they now "hated to go to work."

Through repetition, their very specific response to hearing "just one more thing before you go" had globalized into the all-encompassing "other-blaming" (aka labelling) of "My boss is a manipulative jerk!" They learned tools for dealing with their responses in the specific instance; however, they currently lack tools to deal with the effects of the labelling.

The central message of this Advanced Studies Section is: if you hear yourself referring to someone as "my arrogant boss" (or "my distracted sibling," or "my always-angry parent," or "my impulsive teenager," or, "my always-policy-quoting friend," or "my show-off office colleague") and wondering *What can I do to change them?* you should recognize that other labelling as the warning bark of your guard dog. The bark warns that, having misidentified the problem as being some global attribute of the other person themselves rather than your response to some specific action of theirs, you risk responding stupidly. (Consider if you were the worker discussed above. Once again called to the front office and hearing no warning bark when you react to your labelling them as a "manipulative boss," you decide that it's finally time to take a stand. Immediately upon entering, you blurt out, "I'm sick and tired of your using that 'One more thing before you go' act of yours to manipulate me. We both know it's just a ploy you use on everyone who works for you so they can't question your decisions. I won't put up with it anymore." After a moment your boss replies, "I don't know what you're talking about; I only called you in to tell you that you were getting a raise for the quality of your work." Had you heard the bark and taken time to think, you might have identified your proximate problem as actually being how you were feeling about being called to your boss's office and used quality decision-making to reach a more desirable decision and make a less intemperate opening statement.)

In short, because such "other blaming/labelling" will lead to making stupid decisions, treat its appearance as a warning bark. Take time to think before deciding; it's warning that you are about to act based upon a globalized response to some often-repeated original trigger (e.g., "Why is she still asking me if she can wear make-up when we've been over this a hundred times!"), rather than basing your actions on quality problem solving.

Supporting this message, the following key learning points will be elaborated later in this section:

- Your labelling may be simple hyperbole.
- The other person is unlikely to have repeatedly and deliberately done something simply to irritate you; however, they easily could have been oblivious to your feelings.
- The same factors that can make it difficult for you to hear your guard dog's warning barks can affect them in a similar way; however, the concept of a warning bark which you learned by

studying earlier portions of this book may be completely foreign to them.

- You cannot unilaterally tame someone else's stupid monster; therefore, reducing the burden of their decisions/actions on your life depends entirely upon how you respond when they repeatedly pursue decisions/actions tempting you to blame or assign labels to them personally.

Even at this "Advanced Studies" level, this is still about you, reader, and how effectively you can deal with your Stupid Monster; your child might repeatedly act arrogantly, but their repeated actions do not require you to repeatedly act stupidly.

TO DO NOW

1. Identify the person with whom you interact regularly and whose actions make you ask yourself over and over again (some variant of), "How can they possibly be that stupid all the time" AND WITH WHOM you are most eager to interact more effectively in the future.

2. Identify as best you can an apparent "common trigger" for your response. (Does a specific topic "bring out their stupid?" Does a specific location or setting do so? Does it follow a certain action, comment, or response by them or by you?)

Individual	Common Trigger

3.   Read the following two case studies; each contains two scenarios in which someone's view of another's repeated actions as being "wrong" has led them to mentally assign a pejorative label from the decision to the decision-maker.

Case Study One
Beach Week

Seven high school seniors (three boys and four girls) want to participate, unsupervised, in this year's "Beach Week" following their graduation. They plan to jointly rent a cabin for the week, share food costs, and generally "have a good time" before they leave home for college, jobs, or the military. Beach Week has gone on for many years, and, while it sustains a reputation for widespread alcohol abuse, drugs use, and sexual encounters, local police and civic leaders downplay their impact. Examine the two separate scenarios that follow:

Scenario A:

- At the dinner table, one of the teens announces, "Mom and Dad, seven of us are going to rent a place for Beach Week; I'll need $400 for my share of the rent and food."
- In response, a parent says: "That's just another of your stupid ideas. As long as we're still paying your bills, you can't go."

Scenario B:

- As soon as the teenager comes into the house, one parent announces, "James' parents just told us about this Beach Week thing; we don't want you even thinking of going; we won't let you."
- In response the teen says, "You two are always so controlling; you don't let me do anything, even though I'm already eighteen!"

Case Study Two
"Can you do me a favor?"

A supervisor regularly tacks the phrase "One more thing before you go; can you do me a favor?" onto encounters with a subordinate and follows it with previously undiscussed instructions for different actions. Called to the supervisor's cubicle, the subordinate is already angry that their arrogant boss "will again be manipulating me like this." Examine the two separate scenarios that follow:

Scenario A:

- After hearing a favor request as they anticipated, the subordinate realizes that to do exactly as requested this time might have significant negative consequences, but they are certain their "arrogant boss" never bothered to even consider possible consequences before issuing yet another "instruction, disguised as a favor request."

Scenario B:

- No favor request occurs, but the subordinate leaves the cubicle still feeling the effects of residual anger towards their "stupid boss who is always trying to manipulate me."

TO DO LATER

At the end of this Advanced Studies Section, you will be asked to apply your new insights into evaluation of these four scenarios. You goal will to be able to peel from the decision-maker the other-blaming label and to identify actions you can take that will make desired outcomes more likely.

CHAPTER SEVEN

RECOGNIZING THE
WARNING BARK

By now, your stupid monster taming skills should be sufficiently robust that you understand that a generalized response towards your "arrogant boss." distracted sibling," always-angry parent," "impulsive teenager," "always-policy-quoting friend," "show-off office colleague" is actually a warning bark of your guard dog trying to alert you that you seem about to undertake a potentially stupid action/decision.

When you feel a generalized response like, "I'm angry because my Dad is such a jerk," if you recognize it for what it represents (labelling/other-blaming), you can then employ your new stupid monster taming skills to search for, evaluate, and implement alternative actions/decisions.

It sounds so easy! Why, then, is it so difficult? Why is this considered "Advanced Studies," rather than just as another "tell" to be recognized? The big difference is that here you are hearing a warning bark triggered by the already completed action/decision of *someone else* rather than being triggered by an anticipated action/decision of yours.

Part of the difficulty arises from the temporal connection. We are accustomed to a temporally immediate cause-effect relationship for our tells. For example, before proceeding after a stop sign, I know from experience that a certain odd discomfort is a warning to check right and left before entering the intersection. That same discomfort, when it occurs as I approach a dark alley while walking a deserted street at night, is warning me to cross to the opposite sidewalk right now. The warning bark is proximate in time to the contemplated decision; it does not occur hours ahead when I am thinking about driving to the market or considering a nighttime walk to the bus stop. Such close temporal linkage characterizes most of the warning barks discussed in prior chapters; it's what we are used to experiencing.

Contrast that with the feeling of generalized dread felt by a worker anticipating being called to the office of a boss they globally describe as "arrogant and capricious." That "tell" may occur many hours prior to the actual event.

A second portion of the difficulty derives from the usual close linkage of a warning bark to a *specific* contemplated decision. In the above examples, my odd feeling is generated by the specific decisions under consideration; it is not an unfocused response to all aspects of driving, or all types of sidewalk behavior. These two examples are closely linked temporally and substantively to the considered decision. The rather unfocused anger expressed as "my Dad is such a jerk!" (or similar labelling of others) is quite different. It is neither temporally nor substantively related to any pending decision. Why, then, do I urge you to treat it as a warning bark? Of what is the bark warning you?

It's warning you that you have stopped responding to actual events and have descended a slippery slope:

- First comes your reaction to someone else's specific action/decision ("I'm mad at my Dad because he just announced that I can't wear makeup until I'm fifteen; that's stupid.").

- Next, the reaction becomes directed at the repeated nature of the action/decision rather than at the specific action/decision itself ("My Dad's a jerk who keeps saying over and over again that I can't wear makeup until I'm fifteen; I heard him the first time.").

- Finally, the response becomes globalized; separated from the specific action/decision, it is now operative even absent a specific action/decision. ("Here comes my jerk of a dad; everything he does makes me angry.") What previously was an adjective describing the other person (My "dad who can act like a jerk") has become part of a compound noun representing that person ("my jerk Dad"). That compound noun becomes your generic response to any action/decision of the person with which you disagree ("I'm so mad. My jerky Dad is at it again."). By now, what had once been your response to someone repeatedly acting/deciding something you specifically felt to be undesirable has become a global anger in response to a compound noun straw man of your own creation ("I'm almost always mad at my stupid Dad.").

The warning bark (your creating such a compound noun straw man) should alert you that while you are reacting negatively, you are likely to have, at best, an incomplete understanding of the origins of your negative reaction. At this point, you likely cannot accurately state your proximate problem. Absent an accurate understanding of the proximate problem, the quality decision-making skills you practiced in earlier sections of this book (Pages 55-70) are unlikely to be effective. If you ignore the warning bark, you are at high risk of a butt bite.

TO DO NOW

Identify recent occasions when you have globalized your responses to the actions or decisions of two different individuals by creating and using a compound noun straw man to describe them.

Individual	Compound Noun Straw Man Assigned
1.	1.
2.	2.

TO DO LATER

For each of the two occasions identified above, analyze in some detail the sequence that occurred whereby you globalized from concern regarding a specific action/decision of a third party to characterizing the third party using a compound-noun straw man. How did you "get there?"

Occasion 1:
Occasion 2:

CHAPTER EIGHT:

DISCERNING THE WARNING BARK'S MEANING

Imagine you are angry at your boss and you realize that in your mind you have identified them as your "intellectually dishonest boss."

Congratulations! You have recognized an important type of warning bark rom your guard dog! Now what?

With a little thought, you can place this warning bark into one of three categories.

- It is alerting you to a single decision which you feel is intellectually dishonest.

- It arises from repetition on many occasions of what you feel is the same intellectually dishonest decision.

- You cannot identify any single decision that triggered your response; you just have come to regularly identify your boss by the phrase "my intellectually dishonest boss."

The first type of warning is the easiest to recognize and to react to in a positive manner; success requires only deployment of skills you learned in the earlier portion of this book. Your guard dog has warned that you are at risk of responding to the decision/action of someone else (a decision that you view as so obviously intellectually dishonest that you transiently extend the label of intellectually dishonest to include the person as well as to the decision) by making your own stupid response.

Say a Mom suggests she accompany her teenage son or daughter on a shopping trip for school clothes. The teen's response with some variant of "That's about the dumbest suggestion I've ever heard you make!" is unlikely to lead to the best possible outcome.

Instead, if the teen hears their guard dog's bark, they can use their new skills to analyze how best to respond to this timely warning. They can:

1. Take a little time to think the situation through before deciding. There is (almost) always time to think (see page 216), and then

2. Follow the analysis sequence described in Appendix One-A, page 216. A thought-through response of, "Mom, we could do it that way, but I worry that if we did, I'd never learn to shop for myself. If I go on my own and buy something terribly wrong, we could always take it back. Am I missing something?" may better serve the

teen's purpose of buying their own clothes without real-time parental supervision.

The second and third types of warning are different, and an understanding of those differences is essential to identifying and implementing a decision likely to have a desirable outcome.

In the second type of warning, as in the first, you are able to identify a clear linkage between someone's specific action and your response; what's different in this second case is that you have permanently converted the adjective (impulsive) describing the act/decision itself to a compound noun straw man (impulsive teenager) representing the person repeatedly acting/deciding in this way. You now view them as being personally impulsive because, over and over again, they act/decide in a manner you view as impulsive. You now view them, not their repeated acts/decisions, as the problem.

For example, a father finds the family car in the driveway almost out of gas again. Having provided the teen with a gas credit card valid at the 24x7 Quick-E-Mart down the street, and after having reminded them of their responsibility to always leave car with the tank at least half full following each of the multiple tank-empty occasions, the father now says to himself, "How can Pat be so irresponsible all the time!" However, having studied the Advanced Studies precepts of this book, a warning bark alerts the father to the likelihood that a response of "Pat. You are always so irresponsible!" is probably not going to solve the ongoing problem of the car's almost empty gas tank. The father's problem is not that Pat is irresponsible in general, but that Pat repeatedly acts/decides in a specific way the father characterizes as irresponsible. The repetitive nature of the action is the problem, not the outcome of a single instance of the action. Instead, a response of, "Pat, the car's tank is almost empty. I'm afraid driving it now will just suck tank sludge into the carburetor. Would you take the gas can from the garage, fill it at the Quick-E-Mart, pour it into the car's tank, and then take the car back and fill the tank," is likely to better address the proximate problem, which is the act and not the person.

The third type of warning has a far more complex origin. Here, the action/decision that triggers your guard dog's bark is entirely within you. You have come to identify someone exclusively by the compound-noun straw man you created to represent them. While you cannot identify any specific reason for this generalization, you respond towards them based upon this permanent label that you have affixed. Once this happens, your response is to this compound-noun straw man rather than to a specific actions/decision of theirs (either isolated or repetitive).

For example, a worker finds that every time they speak to their boss, they feel sick to their stomach (a warning bark). They might explain this response as "because their boss is a total jerk who just always hands out more blame or more work!" They are not reacting to any specific or repeated actions/decision; they explain their own unfocused anxiety on the basis that their boss is "just such a jerk."

In fact, reliance on this type of globalization can eventually:

- Result in a Pavlovian-like response where simply thinking about the boss triggers anxiety (Every time I think of that jerk, I feel like I'm going to be sick to my stomach.").
- Extend to entire groups of people ("Those headquarters suits are so stupid they couldn't even find their butt with both hands and written instructions!").

When you hear yourself explaining your response using a compound noun straw man, recognize that is a warning bark from your guard dog. Examine your response and determine which of the three categories described above best describes its origins. If it originated in the first category, you already have the skills to deal with it successfully. If its origins lie in the second or third category, reading the next two parts will provide you with new skills adequate to dealing successfully with the warning bark and to avoiding butt-bite.

TO IMPROVE NOW

From your past experiences, identify an example of each of the situations below where you applied a compound noun as representing an individual either for a single or repetitive action/decision.

Decision Type	Specific Act/Decision That Triggered Your Attribution of "Stupid"	Person Making Triggering Decision
1. Single stupid decision		
2. Repeated occurrence of same stupid decision		

TO IMPROVE LATER

1. Describe your analysis and your decision in the single action/decision above. How easy (or difficult) was it for you to identify and employ the applicable skills from earlier in this book?

2. Later in this Advanced Studies Section, you will return to analyze the second case above and work through appropriate actions/decisions to avoid butt-bite in dealing with it.

CHAPTER NINE

WHEN THEY DO THE SAME STUPID THING OVER AND OVER AGAIN

"When he did that once it was irritating, but what's really infuriating is that the idiot keeps doing it over and over again, no matter what I do." All of us have had similar thoughts on multiple occasions.

You could easily make such a statement as a parent describing an interaction with their teenager, as a teenager describing an interaction with their parent, as a friend describing an interaction with another friend, or as a frontline worker describing an interaction with their supervisor.

Careful examination of the opening statement reveals that two distinct triggers coexist. First, you have responded to an individual action/decision, and second, you responded globally to an action/decision that has occurred over and over regardless of your actions. In isolation, you viewed the action/decision itself as idiotic:

"It's idiotic of them to do XYZ over and over again." As they repeated the same ill-advised action/decision multiple times, you objectified the adjective. Now, "That idiot just did XYZ again!"

Each such trigger presents you with a separate problem you must solve to avoid making an ill-advised response yourself. While similar, the two problems are not identical:

- The first problem is: "How do I effectively respond to this single instance of the action/decision?"
- The second problem is: "How do I effectively respond to this same action/decision that is being carried out over and over again?"

By parsing the situation you originally faced into these two parts, you can use Stupid Monster avoidance skills already learned to deal with the first: responding to this single instance of the stupid action/decision. Again, attention to your guard dog's warning bark allows you to take time to think, apply appropriate problem-solving techniques, and identify and implement an appropriate response. Thus, in the short run you can sidestep the need to expend time and effort cleaning up after the undesirable consequences of an action/decision; instead, you can spend the time thus saved to analysis of the situation's second part:

responding to this same ill-advised action/decision being reached over and over again.

A common mistake is to view the repetition as being your problem, and therefore, to state your goal as "changing the person's behavior so that they don't take that same action/decision over and over again." While that goal appears superficially appropriate, actually reaching it would require the other person to learn to act/decide differently; would require you to serve as their teacher; and would require them to assume the role of student.

For participants in a parent-teen, friend-friend, or worker-supervisor pairing, attempts to create such a teacher-student relationship are generally extremely uncomfortable and rarely effective. (One time, I carefully described to a supervisor how the tiny savings resulting from their regular rejecting small expense claims of sales staff for legitimate but receipt-less cash expenses that amounted to less than $25 per man per month were not worth the resulting animosity. I recommended a change in the corporate policy, and my supervisor dismissed me by responding, "Barry, the requirement for a receipt comes from corporate; if corporate wanted you to teach them how to run this business, they'd have asked for your help!")

More effective is to accept that actually, your problem is not the other person's action/decision; in fact, your problem is avoiding a stupid *response* to the other person's repeated ill-advised actions/decisions. (Yes, your problem might resolve were the other person to permanently change their behavior, but they are unlikely to be a willing pupil even were you able to be an effective teacher.)

Solving your actual problem will require you to

1. Hear the warning bark ("I'm characterizing them as stupid because they keep doing this same thing over and over again, and that makes it more likely that I will make a stupid response myself.").

2. Instead, state the problem as, "How can I take the best/least bad action/decision in response?"

3. Apply quality decision-making skills to that problem.

4. Select and implement the best (least bad) option.

In the expense claims situation described above, my actual (proximate) problem was my response. I had signed off on the individual expense submissions as they went forward, but now had to explain each rejection to the involved sales staff member. My supervisor's actions presented me with two equally undesirable options: to "be disloyal to my supervisor" by saying to the sales staff that I couldn't control my supervisor's actions/decisions even though I found them ill-advised; or to "be untruthful" by saying that I agreed with the rejection's rationale and would no longer forward similar requests as "approved." I was angry that my supervisor's repeated actions/decisions placed me in this position; however, by globalizing, I had moved my focus from where it could be effective ("repeated stupid actions/decision by the supervisor") to form a far less effective image ("the stupid supervisor who is taking the same bad actions/decision again and again").

Upon analysis, I was able to identify my problem as *my response* to the position in which I felt placed by my supervisor's actions/decisions. Remembering their earlier curt dismissal of my advice to revise corporate policy, I considered several options. I could:

- Reimburse the sales staff from my personal funds.
- Reimburse the sales staff from my office petty cash funds.
- Tell the sales staff to forge receipts for these small expenditures.
- Seek the assistance of my supervisor more effectively than I had done earlier.

Selecting the latter, I went to my supervisor and said, "I've got a problem, and need your advice. I don't know how to deal effectively with the sales guys. They're angry at not getting reimbursed for their legitimate but receipt-less minor cash expenditures; they see it as 'our not trusting them.' I don't want to be disloyal and just blame 'corporate policy,' but I can't honestly tell them I feel their claims are illegitimate. Given your experience, how do you suggest I deal with how they feel?"

Thus stated, I became the person with the problem; by no longer assigning blame to their decision, that statement identified my supervisor as part of the solution to a problem of mine. This new statement of the problem had the inherent beauty of being both true (I was the one with the problem) and retaining comfortable roles (my supervisor could now serve as my teacher and I could act as their student).

For emphasis, let's re-examine the sequence here: I was able to recognize that my identifying the problem as my working for a "stupid supervisor" was actually a warning bark; further, I was able to identify that this globalized view of my supervisor was the direct result of my response to their repeatedly disallowing sales staff expenses I felt legitimate. I identified that "the" problem was "my" problem. I concluded that I needed to respond differently, so I examined possible options and selected and implemented the option I determined to be the least likely to lead to an undesirable consequence.

Identifying the problem as being "uniquely mine" was the key to its eventual resolution. While I am capable of (and responsible for) bringing satisfactory solutions to "my problems," I cannot unilaterally bring about solutions to problems "belonging to" someone else.

TO IMPROVE NOW

You previously identified (page 197) a compound noun straw man you created because someone repeatedly took the same ill-advised action/decision. In the space provided, describe how your response to that repeated action/decision was followed by an undesirable consequence:

TO IMPROVE LATER

List a minimum of three alternative actions/decisions can you identify that might be less likely to be followed by an undesirable consequence than was the actions/decisions described above:

CHAPTER TEN

WHEN THE PROBLEM BECOMES A STRAWMAN

Permanently transferring (globalizing) an adjective describing a specific ill-advised action/decision (or repeated actions/decisions) to the person taking it (thereby creating a straw man as described on page 196) creates a cascade of dangerous new problems.

Superficially, your reaction to this straw man mimics a reaction to repetition of the same decision over and over again, as described in Chapter Nine. In each case, warning barks should be triggered by your identifying someone by use of such a straw man ("my impetuous sister"). However, while in Chapter Nine you learned to parse out the specific repeated decision you viewed as stupid (and, thereby, to respond effectively), in this case there is no specific action/decision associated with the warning bark. It's only a generic notification ("my impetuous sister is back at it again"). As the following example demonstrates, such a generic notification will not trigger any effective anti-stupid response on your part.

When asked how he is going to deal with his anger over a decision by his mother with which he disagrees, the teenager offers only: "There's nothing I can do about it. It's her stupid fault. She's always stupid like that. She makes me so mad!" He invokes the "stupid mother" straw man both to explain why something happened and to explain his powerlessness to change it.

The teen does not recognize that his invoking of this "stupid mother" straw man is itself a warning bark, and that his having decided that "he can't do anything about it" was, itself, a likely stupid decision portending undesired consequence.

Once created, such straw men can easily block recognition of warning barks whose alerts could have provided time for identification of, analysis of, and selection of alternative decisions. Involving a straw man in this manner is regularly followed by a butt bite that can be (easily and conveniently) blamed on the straw man. ("That never would have happened if she hadn't been so stupid," says the teenaged son.)

My message here is that when the best answer you can come up with to the question "Why exactly are you so upset with them?" is some variant of "Because they are so XYZ all the time," you can be pretty certain you have assigned blame for a problem to a straw man and are unaware of an important warning bark (and a threatened butt bite).

Other indications that you have created such straw men are when you mentally engage with them in anticipation of some hypothetical future decision/action by the other person. Such is the case of the father who dreads coming home from work because "I just know I will have to deal with something my clueless wife has done." Likewise, the teenage daughter who comes downstairs to a family gathering already angry in anticipation that "Mom is going to embarrass me somehow, just because she's always unfeeling like that," has mentally invoked a straw man, totally in the absence of any specific triggering action/decision by the mother. When you find yourself emotionally reacting in advance to some action/decision you anticipate "that XYZ person" will make, a straw man is likely involved and the butt bite danger is elevated.

The effects of these strawmen can become so well established that they overwhelm entire segments of people's lives, even in the absence of hypothetical future third party actions/decisions. Examples include the teenage son who joins the military as soon as he is eighteen "just to get away from my clueless parents;" the parent who dreams of limiting contact with a "silly daughter" by downsizing as soon as she leaves for college; the worker who plans their exit from what had been a dream job because their new boss "is just so toxic that I can't stand it there any longer." When you find yourself emotionally reacting simply to the idea of "that stupid person" in your life (and not to some decision/action of theirs), a straw man is likely involved, and butt bite threatens.

It is important that you be self-aware. Whenever you react globally to a straw man of your creation, rather than to some specific action/decision of another person, you should hear that warning bark and react appropriately. The next section will examine the careful consideration this particular type of warning bark merits.

TO DO NOW

Identify a time in your life when, you are now aware, you created a straw man of the sort and purpose described above.

- What person did the straw man represent? _____ _____

- What adjective did you use in creating this straw man? _____

- List three undesirable consequences that followed your reacting to this strawman rather than to some identifiable action/decision:

  ○ _____

  ○ _____

  ○ _____

TO DO LATER

Examine the three undesirable consequences you identified above as resulting from your reliance upon this model. For each, identify an alternative decision you might have reasonably reached had you understood that the appearance of the strawman actually represented a warning bark of your guard dog and undertaken a quality decision-making process as you now know how to perform.

Alternative decisions:

1 _____

2 _____

3 _____

CHAPTER ELEVEN

HE'S NOT REALLY THAT STUPID, SIR; HE'S MY BROTHER

So what are you to do when your analysis of your guard dog's bark indicates that you are at risk of reacting globally to someone else's action/decision with your personal version of "Just one more thing from that stupid jerk"? What are you to do when you are aware that your globalized reaction is the problem upon which your attention should actually be landing?

Like many things in life, to this question there is both a short answer and a long answer.

The Short Answer

The short answer is always: "Understand that becoming aware that you are using such a straw man is a warning bark from your guard dog; pay attention to it!"

When you hear that bark, your goal is to tease out a single immediate and tangible problem you confront right now as a consequence of your reaction to the straw man. If you can do that, you can go on to employ your already-practiced, high-quality problem solving to deal with it. This will avoid the butt-bite that was likely had you responded reflexively to your reaction to the straw man you created.

This short answer applies in situations where a globalized response is triggered by a third party's specific action, as in the teenager's silent lament: "Dad is such a jerk. Now he says that I can't use the car for a week and he doesn't even remember that I offered to drive my sister and a bunch of her friends to the water park on Saturday so he could go to his softball tournament."

By viewing their father's pronouncement (suspending driving privileges) through their personal (globalized) prism, the teen sees only their "stupid father" straw man. They did not appreciate a bark recommending they take time to think, to identify and evaluate alternatives, and to implement the best/least bad of those alternatives. In fact, their resulting reflexive response of "Dad, you always make such dumb decisions!" will likely make things far worse.

Had the teen correctly recognized their globalized response ("Dad is so stupid") as a warning bark and taken time to think, their subsequent analysis would likely have revealed their immediate problem to be "how to best react to the father's announced decision to temporarily revoke car privileges." While their global belief that "Dad's a jerk" truly is a problem, it is a problem much better dealt with separately and later, after they have responded as effectively as possible to the threatened loss of their driving privileges. The teen would likely be better served were they to take time to think. ("Yes, Dad can be a jerk, and telling him so would feel pretty sweet. However, my goal here needs to be avoiding the loss of my driving privileges.") Thus warned, instead of responding reflexively to their father's pronouncement they might quickly identify alternative responses and select and implement the best/least bad one. (Saying, "Dad, any chance you could change that punishment? If you did, I could keep my promise to drive Sally and her friends to the water park on Saturday" would combine very minimal downside risks with a very large upside potential.

The short path requires:

1. Recognizing that globally identifying someone using a straw man is a warning bark;
2. Accepting that their being such a straw man, while a burden, is not your proximate problem;
3. Identifying the actual proximate problem their decision is causing you; and
4. Applying quality decision-making skills to resolving your proximate problem.

This short path solution is generally adequate for dealing with the actions of those you identify using straw men, but with whom you interact rarely: the "organizational suits" two or more levels above your boss; your cousin in the next state; your grandparents. While it does not address the origins underlying the straw man, since you interact with these people only occasionally that is not a fatal flaw. The individual and aggregate burden of your interacting with them is small.

This short answer path deals less satisfactorily with the issues raised by straw men representing third parties with whom you interact frequently: teenage children, parents, bosses. Because the aggregate burden upon you of reacting to these straw men is huge, taking time to understand their origins and developing skills to blunt their effects is appropriate. Enter the Long Answer path.

The Long Answer

Rather than replacing the short answer, the long answer follows upon it. Requiring considerable mental discipline, this long answer path is not for everyone, but I include it in this Advanced Studies section because it offers the reader a way to deal with their own (often dysfunctional) reactions to decisions of the one or two individuals who most frequently trigger dysfunctional straw man globalized responses (usually a parent, teen, or boss). Here are the steps:

1. Complete the 'Short Answer" sequence by
   a. Recognizing the warning bark, and
   b. Identifying and dealing effectively with the "single immediate and tangible problem you confront right now."
2. Become a detective working to identify the actual genesis of the "single immediate and tangible problem" you just identified. In this role, you face a mystery: notwithstanding your globalized description of them, your (son, daughter, mother, father, boss) is almost certainly not as your straw man personifies them. Therefore, there must be another explanation for the problem you just identified. In fact, three generic possibilities exist for their action/decision:
   a. Their analysis was actually correct.
   b. Their analysis failed to incorporate into their selected action/decision relevant information that is included in your analysis.
   c. As they contemplated this decision, they failed to hear the bark of their own guard dog.

Let's examine each of these three generic explanations in greater detail.

<u>Perhaps their analysis is correct</u>: Your view that someone's action/decision is ill-advised is not automatically correct. Sometimes when identifying their action/decision, the other party defined the problem differently than you did; considered factors of which you were unaware or misunderstood; viewed as relevant certain factors you dismissed as not relevant; valued identified possible outcomes differently than you did and consequently undertook a correct action/decision, while you failed to do so.

The father discussed earlier could have been restricting his teenaged son's driving for a week after finding the car again parked in the driveway with the fuel gauge showing only fumes and considering an earlier agreement between them that the next occurrence would result in a suspension of the son's driving privileges for a week. In such a case, the son's characterization of the father's action/decision as "dumb" is incorrect.

Similarly, if you are unaware of a sudden drop in new orders for your company's products, you may well attribute a decision to not fill vacant positions in your organizational element to a "clueless boss."

Simply accepting the possibility that you could be wrong, that in a specific instance your response may have been incorrect while that of the other person may have actually been correct, benefits you. By focusing your attention on the action/decision and not the individual making that decision, it reduces the overall capacity of a straw man of your creation to intrude into other areas of your life.

The more often the teen considers the possibility that their father may not actually be the "jerk" of their straw man, the more likely the teen will be, when confronted with a decision with which he disagrees, to engage in productive decision-making. The more often a subordinate can stifle a reflex response to their "toxic boss" and consider the possibility that the boss's action/decision might, this time, be correct, the less likely are they to allow the stupid boss straw man to intrude undeterred into other aspects at work.

As I worked to improve my personal Stupid Monster taming skills in my workplace, I found that I could often gain useful insight by stating to my supervisor, "I'm wrestling with how to take better actions/decisions; I know I don't always even recognize all the factors involved; much less their individual importance. Could you help me out by outlining what alternatives you considered and why you took the action/decision you did?" (I did have to practice saying that out loud to the mirror many times before it lost its initial smarminess, but with practice it worked well.) By not directly challenging a specific action/decision and, rather, by appealing to my supervisors' image of themselves as effective mentors, I became better at including their likely point of view in my future analyses.

Understanding that sometimes their decisions were right and mine were wrong lessened my rate of straw man-induced stupid decisions.

<u>Perhaps they failed to consider one or more important factors</u>: While there can be many explanations for why this happens, there can be no doubt that it is common. We have all uttered some form of "If I'd only known that, I'd have done something different!" The father might have modified the driving restrictions had he remembered the water park commitment; the supervisor might have addressed the hiring decision differently had they known that you had already made employment offers to two individuals. Sometimes the overlooked factor is that their decision will upset you. ("I wish I had known beforehand that you would feel so strongly about it, because I probably would have done something else," a supervisor once told me.)

In such circumstances, I have found useful statements along the lines of: "I have some information that might bear on your decision, but of which I believe you are unaware," or "You probably don't know, but I have some pretty strong feelings on this." Again, such comments require a little rehearsal to get down tone-perfect, but properly presented allow someone the opportunity to gracefully reconsider an action/decision based upon "new" information rather than having to defend that action/decision against frontal challenge.

Perhaps they missed hearing their guard dog's warning bark: Many people have never developed skills to tame their Stupid Monster. When totally unaware of their own tells, such folks have no guard dog, and are unable to avoid stupid actions/decisions. However, as discussed in Chapter Four (*Don't Let the Warning Go Unheeded*) many factors can make it difficult for them to hear a warning bark that was obvious to you. They receive no warning that they are about to take stupid actions/decisions, but you assume that they are deliberately choosing to ignore "obvious" warnings.

Their problem results from their inadequate Stupid Monster management skills; your problem results from your viewing their actions as deliberate. Since you believe that "only a stupid person would deliberately make the same stupid decision over and over again," you create the straw man of stupid teen, stupid boss, or stupid parent as the explanation for their repeated decisions. [This is Social Psych 101: We each make situational attributions for ourselves (such as "I would've thrown my Coke can in the trash here at the bus stop, but there was no trash can"), while making dispositional attributions for others (such as "Look at that self centered jerk, leaving his Coke can next to the bench."). We cut ourselves all the slack and fail to recognize that the same kinds of things are absolutely at play for others.]

As discussed earlier, your creation of this straw man actually increases the chance that you will react stupidly; therefore, in fact, <u>you are reacting to the inability of someone else to properly respond to the bark of their guard dog by doing something stupid yourself</u>; that's a self-inflicted wound!

Here is the sequence I use to avoid such a self-inflicted wound:

1. Decide you will act on the assumption that the person is **not** globally impaired; that you will conduct your analysis on the basis that, instead, they must have not noticed the warning bark of their guard dog.

2. Use the list in Chapter Four (*Don't Let the Warning Go Unheeded*) to identify specific personality traits, behaviors, or settings that might individually or collectively explain the person's blunted response to that bark. (Feel free to add others to the list based upon your personal experiences.) Your goal here is to establish a reasonable hypothesis as to the personality trait, behaviors, or setting that reasonably explains why the other person might not have heard a warning bark, and, as a result, have taken an ill-advised action/decision. My personal experience indicates that the following are common culprits:

a. Impulsiveness of youth (see page 34): Teenagers have the bodies of adults, but their yet incomplete brain development means they generally have less ability to weigh risks associated with various possible decisions and fewer restraints against acting impulsively than do adults. When I find myself criticizing a teenager's actions/decisions ("Couldn't you see what was obviously going to happen?" or "Why did you just go off half-cocked?" or "You had at least three better alternatives to choose from!" I must work hard to remember that the best answers of their yet-to-fully-develop brains may well be: "No; I didn't even think of that possibility," "It just seemed only the thing to do," and "It seemed like the best thing to do." Your blaming the teen for poor action/decisions resulting from these limitations is counterproductive.

b. Unexpected events (see page 48): Parents judge the actions/decisions of their teens to a large extent on the basis of their current (adult) evaluation of their own actions/decisions as teenagers. Through the viewfinder of their fully developed adult brains, the parents now appropriately regard many of their own decades-old actions/decisions regarding drugs, sex, and rock-and-roll as having been "stupid" or "risky;" they fail to understand that the same faulty risk assessment capability of the yet-to-completely-develop teenager's brain that blocked out the advice of their own parents now clouds the judgement of their teenager. Teenagers brains are unlikelyt to acurately incorporate even often repeated and absolutely valid parental warnings. (No matter how experience-based it may be, a parental admonition; "Take it from me, you can get in a lot of trouble if you mix alcohol and sex!" rarely changes a teen's behavior towards either.)

c. Arrogance (see page 35): Arrogant supervisors rarely benefit from the full exercise of their subordinates' talents. Such bosses "only trust their gut," seek little input from subordinates (or fail to incorporate such input) before reaching decisions, and yet frequently attribute undesired consequences to the actions of others. (It's practically impossible to unhesitatingly support a superior whose typical response is along these lines: "Jenkins, you cost us that sale. You're going to it my way from now on.")

Sometimes potential explanations for their response are obvious; when they are not obvious, I have found it very helpful to put myself in their shoes and ask, "If I had failed to hear my guard dog's bark in a similar setting, what would be the most likely explanation?"

3. Re-assess your response to the person's action/decision in light of this newly identified possible explanation. Ideally you will find that your response changes from, "I expect my stupid boss (or teen, or parent, or friend) to keep taking that same action/decision over and over again," to "They keep taking the same stupid action/decision because they can't hear a warning bark; but that, itself, doesn't mean they're globally stupid." That change should be liberating. Rather than being confined to simply reacting to the latest repeat, you can now identify interventions that might lessen the likelihood of yet more "Groundhog Days" in your future.

4. For example: The teen who identifies his response to his father's unexplained revoking of driving privileges as due to global anger might ask himself, "Were I him, what could have made me miss my guard dog's bark?" and thereby identify "anger" as a possible explanation. If the

teen went one step further to ask, "What could have made him angry like that?" he might have remembered the unfilled gas tank and thought to say to the father, "Dad, I didn't notice the fuel level until I was in the driveway, and I was worried it would run dry on the way if I drove the car to the gas station. I didn't know we had a gas can, so I was going to walk there, borrow a gas can, and bring back some gas before you got home, but you got here early."

Globally creating a disparaging straw man representing someone with whom you regularly interact is an invitation to butt bite. Learning to identify that straw man as a warning bark, to tease out the actual proximate issue about to trigger a stupid response from you, and to apply good decision-making skills to identify a better action/decision regarding the proximate issue is a universally wise initial sequence.

By then working to identify a personality trait, behavior, or setting that could explain why the person repeatedly takes the action/decision at issue, you may identify an action you can take to ameliorate the issue in the future.

TO DO NOW

Return to the two case studies on page173. Use what you have learned in this Advanced Studies Section to answer the following:

1. In Scenario A: Draft a different parental response that:
   a. Identifies at least one explanation for the teen's not having heard a warning bark, and
   b. Identifies two specific objections of the parents to "Beach Week" and proposes a route to resolving them in a mutually acceptable manner.
2. In Scenario B: Draft a different teen response that:
   a. Identifies at least one explanation for the parent's not having heard a warning bark, and
   b. Identifies two specific concerns the teen has identified as possible triggers for the parental concern and proposes a route to resolving them in a mutually acceptable manner.
3. Scenario C: Draft a response for the subordinate that deals appropriately with the proximate concern: that the supervisor may be unaware of the possible negative consequences of this request at this time.
4. Scenario D:

a. Write out a hypothesis that could explain personality traits, behaviors, or settings you believe could be causing the supervisor to fail to hear the warning bark their repeated use of this term should generate.

b. Based upon this hypothesis, draft a non-threatening statement you might make intending to encourage the supervisor to choose to behave differently; to stop using that phrase in that way.

CONCLUSION

Taming your Stupid Monster is a marathon, not a sprint!

Reading this book and working through the suggested exercises will provide you with a start, but success over time will only follow from ongoing analysis of the quality of your decisions, along with ongoing evidence-based actions to improve your processes.

Appendix One provides a set of flow sheets summarizing my approach to decision-making when my guard dog barks. I keep a copy hanging over my desk, and I refer to it both when facing a difficult issue and when reviewing a recent failure.

Appendix Two presents a series of items I keep on my smart phone; I also have an alert reminding me each Monday morning to review them and use the phone's notes app to jot down butt-bites soon after they happen.

While seemingly counterintuitive, it will be your occasional failures to avoid butt-bite that offer the greatest opportunities to remain at the top of your game over time. Despite any short-term problems, embrace these as opportunities. Ask family and colleagues to assist you in identifying them; in each case, determine why you failed to hear (or respond to) the warning bark and look for patterns in your failures so that you can revisit the appropriate part of this book, paying close attention to the "To Improve" exercises. They can, after all, be done again and again!

I wish you well on your marathon.

APPENDIX ONE-A:
LOGIC PATHWAY UPON HEARING THE GUARD DOG'S BARKS

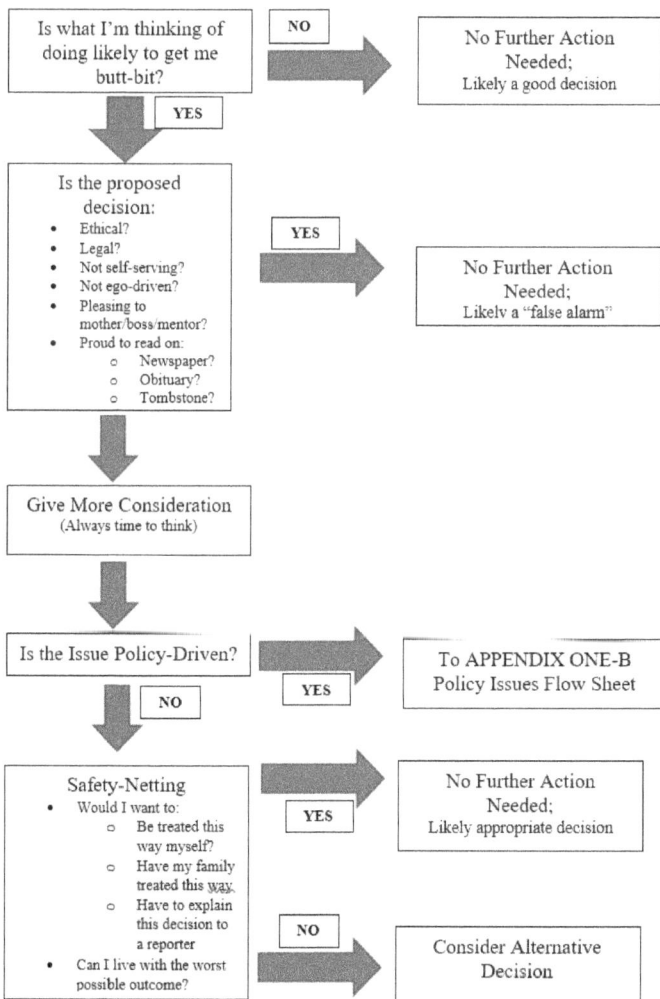

Is what I'm thinking of doing likely to get me butt-bit?

NO → No Further Action Needed; Likely a good decision

YES ↓

Is the proposed decision:
- Ethical?
- Legal?
- Not self-serving?
- Not ego-driven?
- Pleasing to mother/boss/mentor?
- Proud to read on:
  - Newspaper?
  - Obituary?
  - Tombstone?

YES → No Further Action Needed; Likely a "false alarm"

↓

Give More Consideration
(Always time to think)

↓

Is the Issue Policy-Driven?

YES → To APPENDIX ONE-B
Policy Issues Flow Sheet

NO ↓

Safety-Netting
- Would I want to:
  - Be treated this way myself?
  - Have my family treated this way.
  - Have to explain this decision to a reporter
- Can I live with the worst possible outcome?

YES → No Further Action Needed; Likely appropriate decision

NO → Consider Alternative Decision

APPENDIX ONE-B:
LOGIC PATHWAY FOR EXAMINING POLICY ISSUES

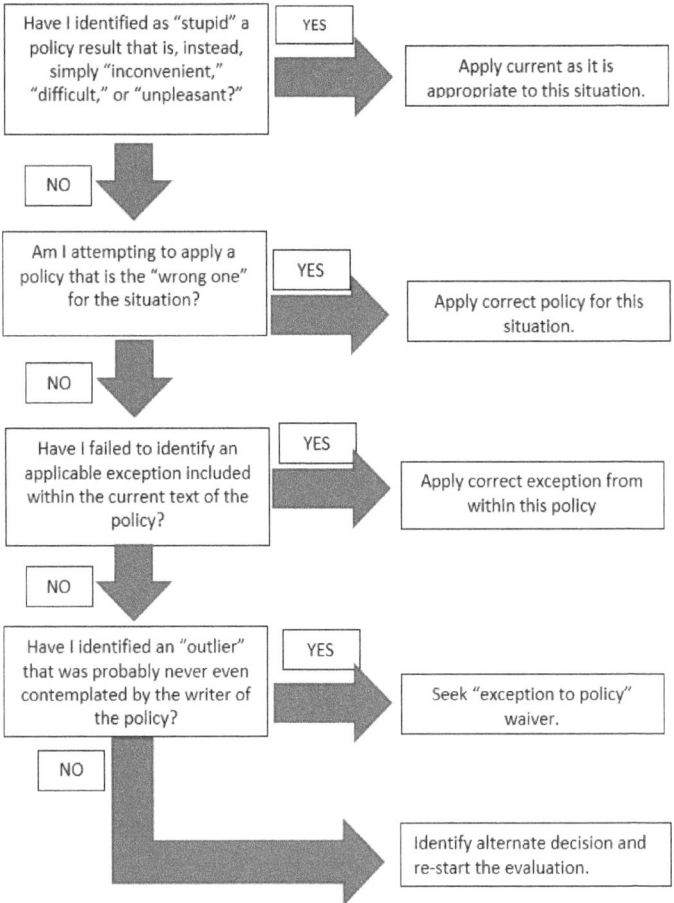

Have I identified as "stupid" a policy result that is, instead, simply "inconvenient," "difficult," or "unpleasant?"	**YES** → Apply current as it is appropriate to this situation.
NO ↓	
Am I attempting to apply a policy that is the "wrong one" for the situation?	**YES** → Apply correct policy for this situation.
NO ↓	
Have I failed to identify an applicable exception included within the current text of the policy?	**YES** → Apply correct exception from within this policy
NO ↓	
Have I identified an "outlier" that was probably never even contemplated by the writer of the policy?	**YES** → Seek "exception to policy" waiver.
NO ↓	Identify alternate decision and re-start the evaluation.

APPENDIX TWO:

KEY POINTS

- There's (almost) always time to think!
- What am I forgetting that I already know?
- Learn to Recognize Your "Tells"
- Beware of:
  - Impulsivity
  - Emotion (anger)
  - "One Last Thing.
- "I can give you the right decision or I can give you a decision right now. You can't have both. Which do you want?"
- Experts are simply information sources.